MINISTERING
TO PRISONERS
AND THEIR
FAMILIES

SUCCESSFUL PASTORAL COUNSELING SERIES

MINISTERING TO PRISONERS AND THEIR FAMILIES

GEORGE C. KANDLE
and
HENRY H. CASSLER

PRENTICE-HALL, INC., ENGLEWOOD CLIFFS, N. J.

The authors acknowledge their indebtedness to the many institutions, both Federal and state, where they have served as prison chaplains. However, the point of view expressed in this volume in no way reflects the official position of the Federal or state government; and the authors accept full responsibility for the opinions expressed.

INTRODUCTION

This series of books represents the most comprehensive publishing effort ever made in the field of pastoral care. These books could not have been published twenty-five years ago, or probably even ten, for the material was not then available. In the past, single books have been available covering different phases of the task. Now we are bringing the subjects together in a single series. Here we present a library of pastoral care covering the major topics and problems that most pastors will encounter in their ministry. Fortunately, not all of these problems need be faced every week or even every month. But, when they are, the minister wants help and he wants it immediately.

These books are prepared for the non-specialized minister serving the local church, where he is the most accessible professional person in the community. It is a well accepted fact that more people turn to clergy when in trouble than to all other professional people. Therefore, the pastor must not fail them.

Russell L. Dicks
General Editor

PREFACE

No single group in America receives so much hostile attention and
so little positive guidance as those who populate our jails and prisons.
The incredible confusion over the modern criminal is not due to
underexposure. Quite the opposite. Virtually every newspaper, TV
network, magazine, and best-seller list portrays tale after tale of cops
and robbers—with murder, larceny, sex, alcohol and narcotics the
shocking subjects competing for attention. It is precisely the sordid
and spectacular character of criminal behavior that presents the
greatest obstacle to viewing the real and troubled people behind the
crime.

This volume directs itself to the point at which the drama usually
closes: the drums stop, the bad guy is overcome and the good guys
shake their heads in triumph and disgust. Attorneys and judges take
over. A sentence is pronounced. Then comes the part we know almost
nothing about. A human being goes behind high walls into near
oblivion. Some distance away his family lives—usually ashamed,
poor, lonely, bitter and isolated.

This handbook proposes a role for the church in the recovery of
prisoners and their families. It is written in the conviction that
momentum is building toward more creative and constructive work
with criminals.

Religion and the law, so tightly bound together in the Bible, are
strange bedfellows to most pastors. For those who wish to connect the
two, this book offers an excursion through the courtroom and the
prison, into the problems of prisoners and their families, to the parish
and prison ministers, and toward the release and return of prisoners
to the free world. The journey details a labyrinth of human tragedy,

social apathy, and institutional inadequacy. The greatest single hope
lies in awakening some vital people in the parish who can reach
beyond their fear of the criminal to the gift of grace that our
religion teaches. That gift, rooted in understanding and in tough-
minded concern, is the focus of this manual.

CONTENTS

CONTENTS

PROLOGUE

February 1. "Bill Stone arrested? I can hardly believe it! What's the charge? Does his wife know yet? Where is she now? Thanks for calling. I'll phone the police right away."

The Reverend Paul Roberts proceeded directly to the County Courthouse. He thought of Pierce Grayson and how convenient it was to have a lawyer in his congregation. Perhaps if he were to call Pierce, he could get some idea of what to expect. Jails, judges, lawyers, trials—it was strange and unfamiliar ground.

As a traveling salesman, Bill Stone spent considerable time away from home. Pastor Roberts knew little about him. He was far better acquainted with Bill Stone's wife, Marge, who attended church fairly regularly. He knew their two sons best.

As the car neared the courthouse, the minister made a silent promise to his God and himself. I'm going to get close to this family—if they'll let me. And I'm going to learn what our church can do for a man under the judgment of the law.

Pastor Roberts arrived after the judge had read the charges against Stone: "You are ordered to appear at this court on Wednesday, March 3. Bail is hereby set at $5,000."

Marge Stone arranged for a bondsman to post a bond insuring Bill's appearance in court. In addition to using their house as collateral, she paid a premium (fee) of $200. Her major expense at this stage was the lawyer's fee of $1,500.

March 3. Appearing in court on March 3, Bill discovers that the evidence against him has already been considered and an indictment issued. Waiving the formal reading of charges, his lawyer requests and receives a copy of the indictment, which reads as follows:

On December 23 at 8:35 P.M. at 599 Eleventh Avenue, the defendant, while armed with a loaded pistol, assaulted Duncan Williams of the Martin-Williams Co., Inc., and stole $2,937 in United States currency. Indicted for:

Robbery First Degree
Grand Larceny First Degree
Assault Second Degree
Criminal Possession of a Loaded Pistol

On his lawyer's advice, Stone enters a plea of "not guilty" to all counts. The case is adjourned to April 17 for a conference and to give Bill's lawyer an opportunity to make legal motions.

April 17. Six weeks later Bill's lawyer, the judge and the assistant district attorney have a conference. Bill does not participate, though he is in the court. The attorneys agree to accept a plea of guilty to robbery, third degree, in satisfaction of the entire indictment. The judge, in imposing sentence, will then take into account Bill's willingness to admit his guilt and will probably impose a more lenient sentence than if Bill were to go to trial.* Bill accepts.

May 4. At the arraignment, the reduced charge of robbery, third degree, is read and Bill offers a plea of guilty. The Judge then sets a date to pronounce sentence. Bill's case (like that of any felony charge) could have gone to trial. Yet his situation is typical in that over 95 percent of all criminal cases are resolved before reaching the stage of trial.**

The legal process is important to Pastor Roberts. He listens and keeps posted as the lumbering legal process unfolds. But his main interest is in the area of pastoral concerns. He asks himself, "What's happening inside this family?"

A host of uncomfortable questions must arise. Can the pastor help the Stones voice them? "What does all this mean to Marge? How does she feel about Bill's crime? Would she, and could she, stick with

---

* This common practice, known as a "negotiated plea" (or "copping out") is a bargain which, in cases where guilt is fairly clear, the defendant saves the State the time and expense of trial in exchange for reduced charges and the promise of a lesser sentence. Such a practice raises ethical questions which are discussed in Chapter IX under "Problems with Sentencing."

** Chapter One offers a chart describing the full process from arrest to trial to incarceration, and a brief definition of several legal terms used in the Bill Stone example.

this man? What about the children? How are they taking it? What's happening to them in school? How is it between them and their Dad? Will they stay in the fellowship group at church?"

And Bill. In the midst of all the paraphernalia of a legal and social defense, there arise the deeper questions: "Why did this happen? What's out of joint—in Bill's spirit; in his home; in his community?" Many violations of the law are the outbursts of people straining under the weight of intolerable social conditions: a paycheck too small; a job too stifling; a problem with alcohol; a house too crowded.

May 18.   On the day of sentencing, Bill's lawyer appears in court and pleads for a lenient sentence. Bill is asked to approach the bench. The judge is direct and firm. "William Stone, you have been found guilty of robbery in the third degree. You are hereby sentenced to be confined in prison for a term of not less than three-and-one-half years nor more than seven years."

A family is now significantly altered. A husband and father is confined. A wife is now fully in charge of the family. Children now know a father who is gone, yet not gone. The law has captured, accused, judged and sentenced not only an offender, but in a different way, his family. For a network of people the verdict is in, and a new page in their life begins.

For those who wish to connect the prison and the parish this book offers a brief excursion through different correctional facilities, into the problems of prisoners and their families; it describes the work of prison chaplains and the opportunities of the parish clergyman; it surveys some of the pressing social and legal issues related to criminal justice, and it outlines basic essentials for a released prisoner's successful return to society. Before approaching the prison, however, it may be useful to devote an initial chapter to some of the principles and practices of criminal law—to gain a broader view of the crucial period between arrest and imprisonment.

MINISTERING
TO PRISONERS
AND THEIR
FAMILIES

CHAPTER ONE

From ARREST To IMPRISONMENT

Nearly 5,000,000 persons a year become entangled in one of society's most complicated processes of social order—the courts of criminal law.*

The Common Law System

The American legal system owes its character to its heritage in English common law. During the English feudal period, each landowner developed his own rules and mores, so that justice varied from manor to manor. With the development of one nation under one king, the transition to one law was an interesting process. Unlike that of other European countries, a single code encompassing all citizens was not written. Rather, it became the practice for judges to reach verdicts based on the mores and customs common to the locale where the crime occurred. In time, this "inductive method" of reaching verdicts in specific cases gave rise to "precedents" which formed the basis for a body of law known as "common law." Thus, the laws were not initially promulgated by a king or a legislature, but grew out of individual judgments which gradually became precedents for the law of the land.

This common law process was well-suited to America with its enormous diversity of national origins. As colonies achieved statehood, they were allowed to maintain a measure of sovereignty over their own law. Thus, even today, each state retains its own penal code. Definitions of crimes, rules of evidence, length of sentences, methods of executions, etc., vary from state to state. What is a crime in one state may not be in another state. For instance, gambling is a crime in New Jersey but is not in Nevada. In addition, there are

* This arrest figure does not include traffic offenses.

Federal laws to account for criminal acts, such as treason, that transcend the jurisdiction of a state.

Civil Law and Criminal Law

It is necessary to distingush between civil law and criminal law. A civil court makes judgments between citizens who have a dispute with each other (e.g., a libel suit) whereas a criminal court makes judgments as to whether or not a citizen has offended the society. In criminal law, if John steals Arthur's car, the dispute is not, as in a civil case, between John and Arthur. It is between John and the society represented by the government.

If a person is suspected of violating criminal law, his arrest may lead to all of these processes—interrogation, hearings, indictment, arraignment, and, in a small percentage of cases, a trial by jury. Approximately three quarters of those arrested, however, are released at some stage in the above process. The remaining one quarter complete the full course of judgment, are found guilty and are then put on probation or sentenced to jail or prison.

The procedure will vary in accordance with the gravity of the offense, a prime factor being whether or not the offense is defined as a "misdemeanor" or a "felony." The distinction between a misdemeanor and a felony reflects the legislature's (and theoretically, society's) feelings as to the seriousness of the crime. Felonies are more serious than misdemeanors and punishable by prison terms of one year and more.

The chart* on pages 22–23 offers an excellent summary of the stages in the process from arrest to prison and definitions of the terms used. Note the two main lines distinguish misdemeanor cases from felony cases. The chart does not detail the very different pattern for youthful offenders.

The Minister and the Law

In our hypothetical example of Bill Stone, there are two simultaneous happenings: a legal process and an emotional experience. On

---

* *The Challenge of Crime in a Free Society*, a report of the President's commission on law enforcement and administration of justice (Washington, D.C.: Government Printing Office, 1967), pp. 8–9.

the one hand, an orderly sequence of legal events takes place between arrest and imprisonment which has important significance for a minister's pastoral work with a man and his family. But the subtleties and variations in this process are endless and pastors cannot possibly be expected to understand the law well enough to give legal advice.

However, even as we caution pastors about giving legal advice, we must stress that ministers can play a valuable role at the legal level in addition to their central role of helping the family cope with the emotional trauma that arrest provokes. There are three specific ways in which a pastor's minimal understanding of the law can serve a parishioner in trouble.

First, he can make the accused realize that laws differ widely from state to state, so that no person in trouble can or should presume that he knows his legal rights and can do without a lawyer. Legal counsel is essential right from the beginning and the pastor can help a person in trouble immediately accept the fact that he must acquire a lawyer regardless of guilt or innocence. The pastor may help select the lawyer. In the many cases where families cannot afford a lawyer, the court will appoint free counsel.

Secondly, a pastor is advised to take nothing for granted in the jails and courts. Jails are usually so overcrowded and court dockets are often so jammed that a person can be lost in the shuffle very easily. A man in trouble with the law needs an advocate as well as a lawyer. A pastor's interest and alertness can do a great deal to insure a man receives proper attention.

Finally, since criminal activities are raw material for newspaper copy, a pastor's active interest in the accused goes a good way to prevent a suspected person from being prejudged by public opinion or political opportunism before the actual trial. As a pastor identifies himself with a person in trouble, he strengthens the purpose of the law by standing against indignant emotional righteousness and standing for unbiased, fair judgment. Often a pastor's phone call to a newspaper editor can be invaluable in appealing to a paper's best motives, and rescue an arrested man from being sensationally prejudged.

Pastoral Care of a Family Awaiting Trial

The *second* thread which weaves itself into the complicated legal pattern is the emotional response such experiences invoke. The pastor

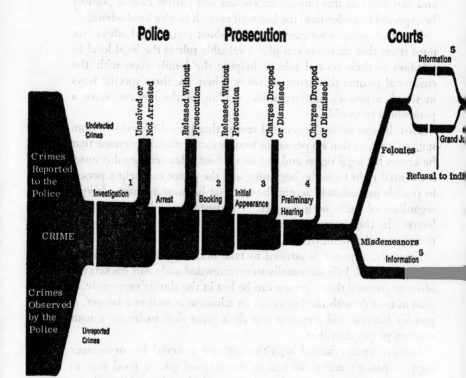

Police **Prosecution** **Courts**

Crimes Reported to the Police

CRIME

Crimes Observed by the Police

Undetected Crimes

Unsolved or Not Arrested

Released Without Prosecution

Released Without Prosecution

Charges Dropped or Dismissed

Charges Dropped or Dismissed

Investigation

1 Arrest

2 Booking

3 Initial Appearance

4 Preliminary Hearing

Felonies

Misdemeanors

Unreported Crimes

5 Information

Grand Ju

Refusal to indi

5 Information

1 May continue until trial.

2 Administrative record of arrest. First step at which temporary release on bail may be available.

3 Before magistrate, commissioner, or justice of peace. Formal notice of charge, advice of rights. Bail set. Summary trials for petty offenses usually conducted here without further processing.

4 Preliminary testing of evidence against defendant. Charge may be reduced. No separate preliminary hearing for misdemeanors in some systems.

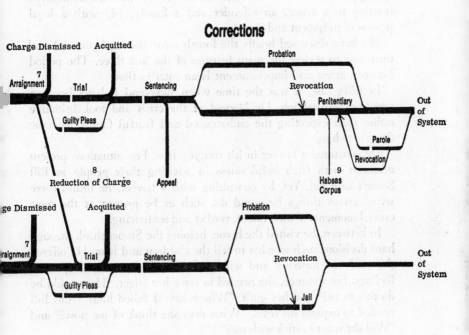

Corrections

Charge Dismissed   Acquitted

Probation

7
Arraignment   Trial   Sentencing   Revocation

Guilty Pleas

Penitentiary

Out of System

8
Reduction of Charge

Appeal

Parole

Revocation

9
Habeas
Corpus

ge Dismissed   Acquitted

Probation

7
rraignment   Trial   Sentencing   Revocation

Guilty Pleas

Jail

Out of System

5   Charge filed by prosecutor on basis of information submitted by police or citizens. Alternative to grand jury indictment; often used in felonies, almost always in misdemeanors.

6   Reviews whether Government evidence sufficient to justify trial. Some States have no grand jury system; others seldom use it.

7   Appearance for plea; defendant elects trial by judge or jury (if available); counsel for indigent usually appointed here in felonies. Often not at all in other cases.

8   Charge may be reduced at any time prior to trial in return for plea of guilty or for other reasons.

will rarely become involved with an arrested person unless that pastor takes the initiative. The Reverend Mr. Roberts did just that, and his involvement led to a concern in four distinct areas: (1) with a man facing prison; (2) with a family in crisis; (3) with a community's reaction to a crime, an offender and a family; (4) with a legal process of judgment and justice.

We have discussed briefly the fourth area (the legal process) and turn now to review the main features of the first three. The period between arrest and imprisonment is an interim time.

In Bill's case, it was the time when Reverend Roberts began a sensitive pastoral job. He learned of the crisis and took initiative rather than expecting the embarrassed and fearful family to come directly to him.

He consulted a lawyer in his congregation. Few situations present ministers with such helplessness in advising their people as Bill Stone's case did. Yet, by consulting with a lawyer, he found there were certain things he could do, such as be present at the most crucial moments of indictment, verdict and sentencing.

In between, he visited the home, helping the Stones think through hard decisions such as what to tell the children and how. He offered the confused husband and wife each the chance to voice painful feelings. For instance, she needed to voice her anger, "How could he do this to us?" and her guilt, "Where have I failed him?" And Bill needed to express his fears, "What does she think of me now?" and "Will she want to stick with me?"

On another front, this pastor was a representative of the Church of Jesus Christ. His attitude demonstrated the meaning of the Christian Gospel. Fundamentally, he represented *acceptance* of a man and a family in trouble. The Stone's discovery that the spiritual leader of their congregation stood with them in their ordeal enabled them to see the church as a source of support. And that vital message would reach each member of the congregation and many in the community.

The pastor's example was not one of judgment or ostracism. The law would seek justice and fix penalty. The church's task was care and understanding. As the congregation follows its pastor's example, the concrete meaning of redemption would make itself felt. A whole family would feel the Christian translation of the words:

Those who are well have no need of a physician; but those who are sick. I have not come to call the righteous, but sinners to repentance.

(Luke 5:31-32)

From now on, therefore, we regard no one from a human point of view; even though we once regarded Christ from a human point of view, we regard him thus no longer. Therefore, if any one is in Christ, he is a new creation; the old has passed away, behold, the new has come. All this is from God, who through Christ reconciled us to himself and gave us the ministry of reconciliation; that is, God was in Christ reconciling the world to himself, not counting their trespasses against them, and entrusting to us the message of reconciliation. So we are ambassadors for Christ, God making his appeal through us. We beseech you on behalf of Christ, be reconciled to God.

(II Cor. 5:16-20)

The period between arrest and imprisonment is a highly charged, painfully dramatic time. It is a time when meaningful and lasting relationships are formed between a pastor, a family and members of a congregation. With the pronouncement of sentence, one period ends and another begins. The guilt is determined and the punishment fixed.

During the period of confinement a new and different pastoral responsibility begins. At this point ministers will be tempted to quit, perhaps even to forget the Stones. The family itself may withdraw into social anonymity and into poverty. Furthermore, the prisons loom as dark and mysterious images. Pastors may feel helpless and it will be easy to dismiss Bill Stone by saying, "At least there is a chaplain there to look out for Bill."

But those who continue to care for a prisoner and his family will face nagging questions and difficult evaluations: a home temporarily without a man; a man who is abnormally isolated; and an ancient, complicated, exasperating system of laws, courts, punishments and prisons.

We must begin somewhere, so we will start with the prison itself—what is its purpose and what is its character? From there, we will work outward to the prisoner, his family, the church, and the host of forces that touch the prisoner's life.

CHAPTER TWO

ANATOMY Of A CORRECTIONAL SYSTEM

A prison serves two basic purposes. The first, *custody,* is the isolation of the offender from society. The second, *rehabilitation,* is the attempt to help him change his antisocial ways. All prison functions are designed to achieve these two fundamental purposes. Men are punished (there's a court system within the prison), but punishment is in the name of custody. Men work (prison industries are sometimes million-dollar operations), but productivity is in the name of rehabilitation. The responsibility of a prison staff is to keep the man safely confined for a given time, and in the process, to mold him into a better citizen.

Most prisons are 99 percent effective in the first purpose, but alarmingly ineffective in the second. One reason prisons do little to rehabilitate men is that we understand too little of the criminal. A second reason is that there are nine persons working at maintaining the prison community for every one person working at altering the prisoner. A recent survey by the National Crime Commission reports that 90 percent of the personnel working in state and local correctional institutions are administrators and guards. 3.6 percent are treatment staff and 5.9 percent are engaged in academic and vocational work.

The Prison Staff

A prison has two staffs: a correctional force and a civilian staff. The correction officers must work in shifts around the clock. Their functions include manning the towers, guarding the men, moving them smoothly from place to place within the prison, checking their cells, their packages, their mail, their visitors, and reporting their infractions. They are custodians of order and obedience. Their whole job is geared to watching for trouble—a difficult, negative and tedious assignment.

The civilian employees, a more diverse group, are usually distinguished by absence of uniforms. They are guidance counselors, parole workers, business managers, secretaries, industry personnel, shop foremen, maintenance men, teachers, doctors, psychologists, dentists, hospital personnel and chaplains.

Both uniformed and civilian personnel have obligations to the work of custody and rehabilitation. Many times a good correctional officer is the best counselor a prison has; while a harsh teacher may be the toughest disciplinarian on the staff. But the two jobs—custody and rehabilitation—can be distinguished from one another. What must be noted at the start is that between them, there often develops a powerful and pervasive tension. Security requirements often block rehabilitation; what is necessary to rehabilitation often interferes with security.

This tension between security and rehabilitation should be kept in mind during any discussion of a prison program as it is a major factor in understanding the experience prisoners undergo during incarceration.

Types of Penal Institutions

A pastor approaching a penal institution should first be aware of the particular kind of institution he is encountering and the type of prisoner who is there. He should also learn whether or not there is a resident chaplain and, if so, solicit his guidance.

Institutions may be described in terms of their auspices, the degree of security, the age limitation, and the program specialty.

Auspices. Federal, State, County and City. Every level of government operates some correctional facilities. Following is a brief description of each.

The Federal Government: There are some 30 Federal penal institutions in the United States, with their total population fluctuating between 20,000 and 24,000. Two Federal institutions confine women. Supervised by the Federal Bureau of Prisons in Washington, D.C., Federal prisons are located throughout the entire country. They can be distinguished in terms of the degree of security, age range of prisoners and type of program. They have a good reputation for the quality of their program and staff.

State Facilities: State correctional facilities (youth and adult) usually confine those sentenced to prison for a serious (felony) crime. They are geared for permanent living and usually offer some program for men to work and study. They vary widely in the extent of their rehabilitative programs.

City and County Facilities: Large metropolitan counties and cities often have a "workhouse" to confine misdemeanor (under one year) offenders. In addition, there are also jails to confine those awaiting trial, those held on suspicion and those already sentenced and awaiting transfer to a prison. Jails rarely have any program to occupy the confined person's time. Unlike prisons, they are not geared to permanent occupancy. Often very crowded, they handle vast numbers of short-term prisoners—far in excess of state or Federal prisons.

Although there is very little structured programming, there are special opportunities for pastors to help persons in jail. Those awaiting trial or recently sentenced are under great tension and often very eager to talk with someone. Ministerial associations can develop chaplaincy services to jails and reach a great many deeply troubled people. In small towns, such a program can be handled on a rotation basis, with each minister taking a turn. Metropolitan areas generally have a full-time chaplain supported by the Council of Churches.

Age differentiation.   Institutions vary not only in terms of jurisdiction of the prison, but also the age range of the prisoners.

Children's Shelters: May be State or private institutions. Although the age limits vary from state to state, they usually confine children under 16.

Reformatories: Again the age limit varies from state to state, but a frequent grouping is 16–25.

Adult Institutions: Usually establish a minimum age limit of 21.

Degree of supervision.   On the adult level (over age 21), there are generally four types of security institutions:

Maximum Security Institutions: Virtually escape-proof. They confine dangerous offenders, long-term offenders, and those with histories of attempted escape. In the past, practically all prisons were maximum security so that such institutions predominate our prison

tion, consult this chapter and say, "Aha, here will be an excellent place for our church choir to sing." Across town might be a maximum security adult prison and a similar application of the above guidelines might lead one to think, "Well, there's not much that can be done there." In fact, the truth might be exactly the reverse. What is most significant is the kind of program, personnel and policy each individual institution has developed. It is therefore crucial that any effort to relate to a particular institution be done in consultation with the chaplain in residence.

CHAPTER THREE

CAULDRONS Of EMOTION

No national strategy against crime can succeed if we do not restore more
of our first offenders to productive society. The best law enforcement has
little value if prison sentences are only temporary and embittering way
stations for men whose release means a return to crime. Today that
situation is all too prevalent. . . . The task of breaking this cycle must
be part of our program.

> President Lyndon B. Johnson's Message to Congress
> —March 9, 1966

Most of us, conditioned by lurid movies and best-seller novels, hold
strange images of "criminals." When we think of those in prison, it is
difficult not to think of John Dillinger, Baby Face Nelson, Al
Capone, and the terrifying characters of Alfred Hitchcock, Ellery
Queen, Batman, and the Untouchables. Such stereotypes are tragic
distortions of the men who come to be prisoners. There is no such
thing as "the criminal mind" or the "typical criminal."

What factors contribute to the incarceration of most prisoners and
why do over 60 percent of them return to prison on subsequent
charges? We know many come out of an impoverished environment;
yet some come from the best of neighborhoods. Many come from
broken homes, but a considerable number are from quite respectable
homes. Poverty breeds crime, but affluence does not insure immunity.
We believe prisoners suffer from a kind of mental illness, but many
are both rational and perceptive. We might expect a lack of ability,
but we find artists, musicians, businessmen teachers, doctors, engi-
neers—the whole range of vocational aptitudes and capacities in our
prisons.

Although labels and categories have proven deceptive, the pastor
needs some knowledge of the distortions that commonly handicap the
prisoner's life. The following pages present ten traits which are

widespread and recurrent among those in prisons. These factors are not exhaustive and they are by no means limited to those in prison. They are presented in nontechnical language, with brief examples, to reveal the prisoner as a person—a troubled person certainly, but a real person nevertheless. Following each description is a "thought question" designed to raise some of the problems of relating the Christian faith to the inmate's situation.

1. Powerful resentment toward authority. "You can't hurt me, you dirty, lousy cop. Go ahead, do anything you like. You can't stop me. Little gods, you think you're little tin gods." Some people simply cannot tolerate rules or those who represent them. They are driven to resist restriction and regulation. They have fear of and anger toward teachers, preachers, policemen—all who control or confine their freedom.

An 18-year-old was arrested for robbing a gas station. Later, when the judge walked into the courtroom, he stood up and shouted, "What are you waiting for? This whole thing is rigged anyway. You're going to throw the book at me, so go ahead. See if I care."

The young man's fate could have taken various directions. But his uncontrollable resentment toward "them"—the authorities, the system, the big shots—so dominated his mind that he taunted and dared the judge to verify his belief that the world was against him. Later, after receiving a sentence of five to ten years in a state reformatory, he had proven what he needed to prove: "I am a victim of fateful circumstance." For him, there are only two kinds of people: those like himself who have no power; and those, like the judge or the prison guard, who have power. He may never overcome them, but he will wage war for as long as he views life as a conspiracy against him.

Men don't always show this resentment outwardly. Willie was a prisoner who always grinned. No one could remove that plastic smile he used effectively to hide all his feelings. An officer would order him to wash down a corridor he'd washed a half-hour earlier. "Yes sir, o.k. boss," he would say with a big grin. And with his pail full of dirty water, he produced a floor less clean than before. With a smile on his face, Willie fought back in his own special style.

Often, in the past of such a prisoner there lurks a father who beat the youth unpredictably. Other times there is no father; only a mother who never said "No." One man in prison said, "It's funny. The first man who ever told me 'No, you can't do that' and really meant it, was the judge."

A thought for theologians: How do you convey the Law of God to a person who has felt all restraint as cruel, all rules as capricious and all lawgivers to be tyrants?

2. Distorted need for attention. With attention, the recognition or awareness of one's existence by others, usually comes approval, praise, and applause. Men in prison have yearned for attention all their lives, and most of them have gotten it—but not through approval. There is just as much attention in disapproval.

Ron was a master "check artist." He wore $200 suits, sported expensive luggage, traveled by air and taxi, and stayed at only the best hotels. To validate his charade he sent himself impressive telegrams which reported investment opportunities, or urged him to come back to a nonexistent corporation immediately. The tools of his trade were an impressive battery of glamorous surroundings. Everything was done by check; every check eventually bounced. But as long as his timing was good (he paid the bills only when leaving) and his retinue convincing, he was center stage—someone who was somebody: a very sophisticated forger. In one prison after the next, he would also be somebody: a craftsman at deceit.

Jerry was a 21-year-old newlywed who stole food from people's refrigerators and cokes from machines in gas stations. His refrigerator at home was full before he went out on a robbery. But his hunger for attention was not satisfied by his new wife, a young woman far less indulgent than his stepmother had been. After his arrest Jerry had plenty of attention. The newspapers printed his picture; friends worried about him; people came to his trial. For a while it was all very dramatic. He was the center of everything. In prison he would find new ways to get attention, and all would be punitive.

A Thought Question for teachers: How do you help a person who has known only one kind of attention—the frown and the whip—to become interested in another kind—praise and approval?

3. A manhood unproven and uncertain. A man comes out of the prison commissary with both shirt pockets stuffed. One pocket is filled with cigars; the other is filled with bubble gum—a good symbol of his self-image. He does not know whether he is a boy or a man. In prisons, one sees hundreds of clues to the same problem: men uncertain of their manhood.

A clue to such uncertainty is often given by the crime a man commits. Consider the following examples:

Manliness in sex: a man molests a little girl in a desperate effort to prove to himself and his world that he is not really afraid of women. But he is.

Manliness through status: a man steals Cadillacs in a tragic search for a day, a week, as someone big, someone people take notice of.

Manliness through millions: a man sells a quarter-million dollars of phony stock to gullible widows, haunted and driven by the echo of his mother's voice, "You'll never, ever, be anything but a bum like your father."

Manliness through association: a slow, dull, likable guy with no hopes beyond promotion from elevator boy to bellhop is fascinated by a smooth con man who tells him all he has to do is drive the car and he'll share one-third of a $100,000 robbery.

A thought for congregations: Do you have a place in your fellowship where a man who is most uncertain of himself can become more certain? Are your people willing to welcome one whose life has never provided him with a good example of manhood?

4. Looking for the rainbow. "The odd thing is, Chaplain, I was almost there. This was the last job. I had reservations for Buenos Aires on Saturday. I was quitting the racket right after this job. Then the 'Feds' closed in."

Some prisoners live in a cyclic struggle with fate. They view the world with amoral eyes: to them life is luck, which lasts a certain time and then expires. Often they are bored and purposeless people. They crave excitement and are driven to raise the stakes regularly to keep the game adventurous.

"I can't tell you why I took the money. I wasn't even thinking of robbery. It was a loan. All I knew was that horse had to win. I was due. It was the big one for me. If that nag had come through, I planned to put the loan back in the company safe that night, and nobody would ever be hurt. How could that horse do this to me?"

The shortcut. It makes gambling the biggest business in the entertainment industry and an endless breeding ground for crime. Behind this obsession is often the need to see if the gods of fate will pour out great treasures. This is especially true of youth, who have "got to have it, got to have it now, and got to have it big."

Men spend hour after hour of prison "free time" lying on their bunks lost in fantasy about the future. They live in a dream world of wine, women, and luxury. They make no preparations, ignore all responsibilities, and exert no efforts to plan realistically. Their lives are spent in a future that will never come.

Thought Question: Something in modern civilization has provoked a restless urgency in many to hit the big time. Why is it that youth is so tempted to find the big win, to buy a two-dollar ticket to a million-dollar payoff? Is it part of the price of affluence?

5. Failure as a way of life. "Born to Lose" and "Born to Raise Hell" are tattoos burned into the skin of many an inmate. Countless numbers in prison have such incredible histories of handicaps that one wonders how they have survived. Files are full of probation reports with sections entitled "Family History" that read like this one:

Defendant's parents are James Caster, 45, and Lisa nee Rigdon, 42, natives of North Carolina and Philadelphia, respectively. Allegedly married in a religious ceremony in 1937. The defendant's father abandoned the family in 1941.

The mother, anemic, apprehensive and feeble, did not complete grade school. For 24 years she received assistance from the Department of Welfare, during which time she was committed to the Jenkins State Hospital three times as a schizophrenic, and once to Marshland State Hospital as a schizophrenic. She drank excessively. Members of her family have lived with her periodically: one, her brother James Rigdon, died from an overdose of narcotics in 1962. Her mother died in 1953. Following her father's death in 1963, one Peter Freeman moved into the home. The defendant disliked him. A year later, in 1964, after Freeman had beaten and abused her, the defendant's mother was admitted to Jones Hospital Psychiatric Division and on doctor's orders left Freeman permanently. Currently she occupies two rooms at $22 per week in a dilapidated private house on the second floor at 291 East 49th Street and is wholly dependent upon the Department of Welfare.

Men from such homes have failure so deeply ingrained in the fiber of their life that it is honest to remark, "They need to fail." All police stations know the story of the man who commits a series of burglaries very successfully. Then, for an unexplained reason, the burglar takes off his gloves. The fingerprints lead to prompt arrest. Why? Maybe he felt it was time the world knew that *he* was the clever burglar (attention?). Maybe his success was just plain bewildering—even frightening. Many in prison have an unconscious defeatist life-plan that helps them verify again and again that they were "born to lose."

A puzzling letter written to a pastor:

I appreciate all your help in getting me a job, giving me the suits, loaning me the car, and introducing me to such nice people. I'm glad I joined your church. But somehow it was all too good. It actually scared me to see things going so well. I can't tell you why I stole the car. I wish I knew. Please come visit me.

When sincere help and care is so unfamiliar to a person, it can be very frightening to experience. Some persons overthrow good fortune and benefactors because the situation is simply too unfamiliar for them to handle, emotionally.

6. An inner emptiness. Men in prison are often diagnosed as suffering from a form of mental illness known as "character disorder." One of the common traits used to distinguish the "character-disorder personality" is an incapacity to form close relationships. Early years of emotional poverty create a person who seems unable to trust anyone and unable to form any friendships. Such individuals are ripe for addiction to alcohol, drugs, gambling, or other extreme compulsive behavior. They may appear gregarious, but within them a persistent loneliness works strange effects on their lives. Such men come to prison saying:

1. "In the midst of a wild drunk I smashed a guy. I didn't even know his name."
2. "I needed a 'fix' so bad I didn't care what happened or who knew it. I broke into the drugstore in broad daylight."
3. "I blew my whole paycheck and hadn't won a dime. I had to keep playing so I just wrote a bum check."

Underneath, one finds persons who are unable to sustain a good relationship. Loneliness is not met with love, but with liquor. Companionship seems impossible with people, but a poker deck or a bag of heroin provide temporary escape and reassurance. In such people, the criminal offense may not be the key to their disturbance.

Rather, their forgery, their burglary, their car theft are actually the tools necessary to support their own special method of trying to fill a bottomless emptiness.

The problems of alcohol, drug addiction and gambling are exceedingly complex. There is not space here to deal with them at length but two of these subjects are dealt with in separate volumes in this series.*

Thought Question: Where a criminal action is provoked by an addiction, or compulsion, how can society take into account a severely neurotic person who needs therapeutic treatment, while also fulfilling the punitive requirement of the law?

7. Violence. Most of us know the white heat of controversy or the sweaty strain of athletic competitions—both are normal outlets for aggression. Oftentimes the movies offer vicarious release for pent-up aggression. But some persons have lived with violence on such primitive and powerful levels that it influences deeply their patterns of behavior.

It was noted earlier that not all prisoners come from poor, uneducated, deprived backgrounds. Bill Sands, a former prisoner, is a prime example. Born into a prominent family, Sands was the son of a wealthy, politically-powerful judge and a cultured, sophisticated mother. His childhood, troubled in many ways, illustrates the grim consequences of a mother's wrath:

Her usually calm voice had turned into a scream. She was holding a long switch in her hand, and now I saw her raise it in the direction of my nearly naked body. . . . Something hot and sharp struck the side of my left arm and scraped onto my back. I touched the hurt spot with my hand, which was immediately stained with blood. I looked at my mother with horror. Her eyes were alight, the way they looked when she appraised her handiwork on the Christmas tree. But there were strange and terrifying lines pressed into her face. Her soft lips were thinned in frenzy. "Turn around!" she ordered. I hesitated. The whip came down in an arc, leaving a weal across my face.**

---

* Thomas J. Shipp, *Helping the Alcoholic and His Family* (Englewood Cliffs, N.J.: Prentice-Hall, Inc., 1963) and Tommie L. Duncan, *Understanding and Helping the Narcotics Addict* (Englewood Cliffs, N.J.: Prentice-Hall, Inc., 1965).
** Bill Sands, *My Shadow Ran Fast* (Englewood Cliffs, N.J.: Prentice-Hall, Inc., 1964).

Most men in prisons live with memories of violence—done to them or done by them, or both. An anger smolders inside them, fed by scenes of horror they have witnessed firsthand. And when they are provoked (sometimes in the mildest of ways) their defense is primitive. They do not have a marital quarrel and then go bowling. They smash their wife in the head. They do not take a chewing-out from the boss and go home to yell at their kids. Instead, they may steal their employer blind, crack up his truck, or send his wife a threatening note. Their expressions of aggression are direct, not indirect; their reactions are extreme, not moderate. Their emotions are not glowing embers; they are blazing fires.

A man's daydream after work. "Lord God, help me get rid of this heat inside. My boss is a sadist. It was 94 degrees in the shop today and he was just waiting for me to sit down so he could yell at me for loafing. The old lady will kill me if I stop, but I need a cold beer. And I know the boss will be in there. And if I drink a few beers and he looks the wrong way—I'll smash him. Lord, help me walk past that bar and forget it."

A thought about prayer: What is God's answer for those whose early lives reflect an intensity of emotion that modern civilization can no longer tolerate?

8. Fear of people. Those who experience extreme rejection from one or both of their parents learn early to distrust everyone—even those close to them. Deprived and threatened from day to day, they live under the shadow of constant fear. Their distrust breeds patterns of relating to people in endless ploys to keep from revealing their real selves. The world and all who dwell therein represent emotional threats and such persons devote their lives to conquering the people that so frighten them. They may become master confidence men. Deceiving and manipulating people is a way of life entirely consistent with their experience that love and trust are not real and not reliable. They may know how to flatter, how to be humble, how to express sympathy or evoke pity—but such emotions are a charade. People are their enemies: their use of feelings is a weapon to conquer their foe. This is an exceedingly difficult attitude to change because of the prisoner's defensive and distrustful attitude towards even the most sensitive of helpers.

A Thought Question: Theologically we believe God is love, and

God loves man. We believe man is separated from knowing God's love and needs to hear and feel the good news that God loves him. We might say that man's fundamental fear lies in being unloved. Yet some persons have been unloved so plainly and dramatically from the start that they are deeply suspicious of love, and fearful of being loved. How then is the love of God in Christ expressed to those who fear and resent anyone who says or shows he cares?

9. Guilt. One of the strangest phenomena of those who reach prison is the role of guilt in their lives. Some men are so plagued with guilt they cry out to be punished. They will deliberately commit a crime or even confess to a crime they did not commit to fulfill the need for punishment.

On the other hand, some prisoners show no outward signs of guilt, invoking such public outbursts as "this man shows no sense of shame at his callous, inhuman act." When a crime is committed people instinctively feel indignation. They look for tears of remorse, and some offenders will not oblige—like Jake. His father strapped him to a bedpost regularly and beat him with his belt and buckle. Jake had only one defense: he vowed never to give his father the satisfaction of a tear. Perhaps that is why he would not give it to a jury either.

One of the interesting efforts in penology has been the experiments with inmate adjustment boards. Since discipline is a continuing burden for prison authorities, officials have periodically tried turning over judgment and discipline to inmate boards. Aside from the dangers of bribery and inmate pressure, the worst problem with such boards is that inmate rules and punishments invariably become too harsh. Inmates come to fear and resent judgment by peers more than that of the authorities. One of the obvious reasons kangaroo courts are so vengeful is they represent the prisoner's powerful fear and hatred of his own impulses. Consequently the punishments that he metes out to himself (i.e., his own kind) are the most severe imaginable.

The point is that prisoners often reflect a disturbed sense of guilt. At some level of their being, far below their awareness (and often anyone's reach), something has been twisted out of proportion. For some, the experience of punishment is deeply gratifying, providing temporary assuagement of their guilt. For others, the guilt may be there but it is sealed beneath a deep layer of anger, defiance, and stony hatred that will not be penetrated by any demands that they show regret.

Thought Question: How do you preach a message of forgiveness to those who do not wish to be forgiven? And how do you convey assurance of pardon to those who would unconsciously prefer to be punished?

10. Desperate need of structure. Prisons are necessary. They are like tight gloves that fit certain hands perfectly. Though they will never admit it, some men are happier in prison than in the free world. They are comfortable and safe; they are taken seriously; they are insulated from responsibility; they are protected from decision-making and from society. "You know, Chaplain, when I enter that cell each evening, they aren't locking me in. So far as I'm concerned, they're locking the world out. It's the best part of the day."

An article written by a civilian prison instructor for *Holiday* magazine points to this strange attraction between the prison and the prisoner:

One of the great lessons of modern psychology is that human beings will do the most outrageous things in order to assure themselves of being loved. I didn't understand the application of this principle to prison life until fairly late in my prison career. I had seen several students of mine return to prison after vacations outside that ranged from a few weeks to a few months, and had listened sympathetically to their accounts of how small-minded parole officers had "busted" them on technicalities, but I had completely missed the real point until the day a prisoner named Duval returned to San Quentin.

For several months, Duval had been the prize student in a course I was teaching in American literature. He was a tall, well-muscled, well-spoken young man of about twenty-five, diffident in manner, earnest and capable of writing class papers that would not have embarrassed him in college. (Quite contrary to the cartoon figure of the convict as a Neanderthal man, the typical prisoner is more likely to be a young fellow in his twenties who, wearing the regulation blue denims, looks as though he might have just stepped off a Navy base.) When Duval became eligible for parole, his drafting teacher, who had also admired his work, helped him find a job in an engineering office in San Francisco. It happened that I was waiting to pass through the outside count gate when Duval came out, wearing a natty state-supplied "dress-out" suit, carrying a brown-paper parcel of his personal gear and looking, as most discharged prisoners do, worried rather than joyful. (There are two count gates, one inside and one outside the walls. They are never open at the same time, thus discouraging a mass rush to freedom. Connecting them is a gloomy passageway whose analogy to the birth canal has not escaped the attention of prison intellectuals.) I shook hands with Duval, wished him luck and, noting his anxious expression, remarked that I had no doubts about his ability to make a go of it back on the outside of the walls.

A bare four months later I picked up my morning paper to read that Duval had been caught red-handed in an appallingly clumsy burglary of an empty house that in fact had hardly anything in it worth stealing. The story had made page one, because Duval's parole officer had remarked to a reporter how odd it was that a man so 'incredibly talented' would have embarked on such an ill-conceived crime, and the papers had blown this up into a story of genius gone wrong. Several weeks later, while I was on my way inside the prison one afternoon, I saw Duval, newly returned, sitting on the bench in the birth canal between the gates. As we shook hands again, I said I wasn't particularly glad to see him. "Well," Duval said wryly, "I'm not glad to be here either," but what struck me forcefully was that his face denied his words. This time he looked reasonably cheerful and at ease.*

Every prison official knows how this instructor felt. The crucial thing is not that Duval possessed great genius. This only accentuates the mystery. The crucial thing is that men who make excellent adjustment to the prison, in fact become model prisoners, are often the worst candidates for successful release. Their talents shine brilliantly in the prison atmosphere, where they are without responsibility—even for themselves; but removed from the rigid, protective institutional life, they soon get anxious and find an excuse to return "home."

Thought Question: Is it possible that freedom can be so overwhelming to some that we must frankly recognize and admit that they will live healthier and more productive lives in confinement?

Having said all this, the picture still remains incomplete. It is necessary to add at least one further dimension to the already complicated picture: the problem of poverty. The plain fact is many men in prison grew up in pockets of poverty where economic, social and emotional deprivation are so extensive that illegal activity becomes the code for survival. Some children grow up in areas where

* Kenneth Larnott, "Cells as Second Homes," *Holiday* (February, 1966).

every significant person around them steals—including the self-ordained, opportunistic preacher. To describe their behavior as abnormal is to ignore the fact that their whole milieu is abnormal and that they quite "normally," predictably and understandably have absorbed and integrated a sick culture and its way of life.

It's an old cliché that suffering builds character. Psychiatrists know, however, that some suffering builds character disorder. Most of this chapter describes the conflict-producing elements that play a part in character disorder. We must remember, however, that parts of our society are so abnormal that the social illness we abhor in prisoners cannot be attributed to individual intrapersonal conflict alone, but must be connected clearly to the larger social ills we can locate in every ghetto, slum, and deprived section of our cities. It is no lie to say poverty breeds crime—not poverty in itself, but families and cultures that huddle together in pockets of poverty, living on the edge of starvation while surrounded by affluence that seems unreachable through any legitimate means.

The American glorification of "work" simply does not extend to many in the lower classes. An "anti-work" ethic eats at such groups with a cancerous effect. Faith in the nation, the future, the law are absent—and in their stead are a set of impulses that lives only for the moment in the moment. *Thought Question: In a society that has tightly connected salvation and work, how do you motivate persons to work, if working brings them neither pride, profit nor salvation?*

The above-mentioned traits are by no means exhaustive, but they are a fair sampling. They are offered for two very important reasons.

1. To emphasize that prisoners are people. We shall not claim that evil and unconscionable men do not exist. They do. But those in prisons are more often *frightened* than fearsome. What stands out boldly is not their malice but their immaturity. They are less like menacing giants and more like immature adolescents. True, they do things which anger and shock, offend and harm others—but they are not monsters. As you review these few characteristics, perhaps those in prison will seem more real to you as "persons" and not simply "criminals."

2. To point out what separates prisoners from citizens is not a unique set of needs. Surely you noticed something of yourself in the ten traits described. *What distinguishes those who fill*

our prisons is the destructive manner in which they cope with their problems. Their needs, to be sure, are very great; and often their resources are not. But this is true for a lot of people, who do not go to prison. They go into mental hospitals, general hospitals, military service, and other institutions. But those who do go to prison usually begin a downhill cycle that may be charted something like the diagram on the following page.

THE DOWNWARD SPIRAL OF 60% OF THOSE IN PRISON.

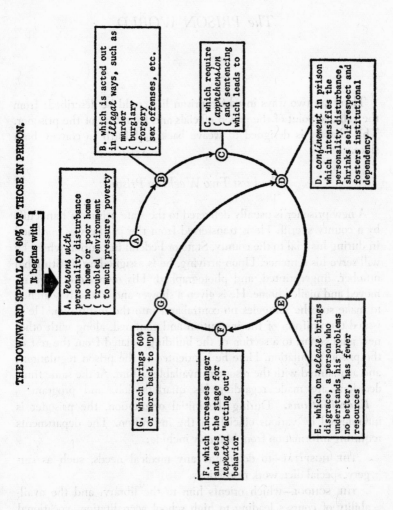

It begins with

A. *Persons with*
personality disturbance
(no home or poor home
(troubled environment
(too much pressure, poverty

B. which is acted out
in *illegal* ways, such as
murder
burglary
forgery
sex offenses, etc.

C. which require
apprehension
(and sentencing
which leads to

D. *confinement* in prison
which intensifies the
personality disturbance,
shrinks self-respect and
fosters institutional
dependency

E. which on *release* brings
disgrace, a person who
understands his problems
no better, has fewer
resources

F. which increases anger
and sets the stage for
repeated "acting out"
behavior

G. which brings 60%
or more back to "D"

CHAPTER FOUR

The PRISON WORLD

There are two ways in which prison life could be described: from the vantage point of the prison officials and from that of the prisoner. This chapter is designed to weave back and forth to convey both sides.

The First Two Weeks in Prison

A new prisoner is usually delivered to the state prison in handcuffs by a county sheriff. He is transferred from the jail he was confined in during his trial to the county, State or Federal institution where he will serve his sentence. Upon arriving, he is assigned an institutional number, fingerprinted, and photographed. His own clothes are removed and mailed home. He is given a shower and carefully searched to make sure he smuggles no contraband into the institution. He is issued the uniform of the institution and confined, along with other new admissions, to a section of the building isolated from the rest of the prison population. Here he is oriented to the prison regulations, and acquainted with the resources available to him. At the same time, decisions are made regarding his quarters, job, and program.

Examinations. During the initial orientation, the prisoner is interviewed by various officials of the institution. The departments requiring information from him may include:

THE HOSPITAL—to determine any medical needs, such as surgery, special diet, work restrictions.

THE SCHOOL—which orients him to the library, and the availability of courses leading to high school accreditation, vocational training, or college work.

THE PAROLE OFFICER—who clarifies such matters as the minimum and maximum periods of his sentence, time given for good behavior, and eligibility date for meeting the parole board.

THE PSYCHOLOGIST—who tests his I.Q. and educational level, and may examine him for emotional illness and recommend therapy.

THE CHAPLAINS—(Protestant, Catholic, or Jewish) who interview him about his religious background, his church preference and, if he has one, his home pastor.

THE GUIDANCE COUNSELOR—who is the inmate's liaison with the outside world. He orients the prisoner to regulations regarding correspondence, visitors, legal rights, and institutional rules.

Usually all mail, incoming and outgoing, is censored, and all visitors are screened and fingerprinted. Most prisons limit the number of correspondents a man is permitted. For example, he may be allowed to write to parents, wife, immediate family and male friends, or a total of eight persons. Married men are usually not allowed to write to any women (other than immediate family) without special permission. Visits are also closely regulated, with rules similar to those regarding correspondents. Institutions, for example, may allow a man five visits per month (although some only allow one per month). A prisoner's minister is always permitted to write and to visit.

The final job of the "quarantine" period lies with a "classification committee." This interdisciplinary group of prison officials interviews the man to determine such things as type of quarters (cell or dormitory), degree of security required, what job he should do, and what special program he should be encouraged to follow. The prisoner's previous record, observations made during his first two weeks, the type of crime for which he is incarcerated, and his personal requests are component factors in the decisions of the classification board. When the process is completed, the prisoner is ready to be transferred into the general population or sent to another prison. His report might read like this:

William Stone	#334-837
Work Assignment:	Mess Hall
Living Quarters:	Cellblock B
Security:	Approved for medium security work.

Medical Recommendations:	Eye cataracts—medical transfer when approved.
Special Program:	Alcoholics Anonymous recommended. 9th grade education; psychologist indicates high school ability. School 3 mornings per week.
Attitude:	Cooperative.

As the prisoner's evaluation and assignments are completed, the process of institutionalization begins. Many new men in prison feel this is the end of individuality.

As pastors visit and correspond with imprisoned parishioners, they often feel caught between what the inmate tells of prison life and what the pastor understands of the institution's purpose. On the one hand, the pastor tours a prison and discovers men have jobs, a counselor, a hospital, a school, a psychologist, a chaplain, a recreation yard and a variety of resources designed for his well-being and improvement. On the other hand, during the pastor's visits the prisoner may disclose experiences which seem outrageous. Somewhere between these two pictures lies the true situation, and that situation varies from prison to prison, state to state, and staff to staff.

The following discussions between Bill Stone and his pastor suggest matters which often come up as pastors visit with prisoners. The goal in these hypothetical conversations is to describe the institutional experience from the standpoint of one prisoner—a first offender and family man. No prototypes are possible, but such "representative conversations" will acquaint a pastor with the environment in which the prisoner lives. To try to balance the prisoner's view with that of the institution, a short comment follows each vignette.

Condensed Conversations Between Pastor and Prisoner

In the visiting room (6 weeks after Bill's admission).
PASTOR: Good to see you, Bill. How are you getting along?
BILL: I'm making it, I guess—the first few weeks were horrible but I'm starting to catch on to the system. Something's happening to me, though, and I don't know what it is.

PASTOR: You mean you're changing, Bill?

BILL: Well, in a way—though I feel more like I'm being changed than changing myself. I've never felt so "second-class." Of course, nobody in this place is "first-class" unless they're wearing the officer uniform. I'm just a number, you know, 334–837. I mean I didn't expect hotel service, but it's this feeling of being dirt, of being scum of the earth, that gets me.

PASTOR: Is there brutality, Bill? Are you being mistreated?

BILL: Naw, I haven't been beaten up or anything. Fights break out but I've stayed clear of that so far. This isn't physical, Pastor; it's different. It's being a nobody and having no respect. We all get the same haircut, we all wear the same uniform, we all write on prison stationery, you know, those lined papers I send you—we're all inmates and that means we're all liars, cheats, thieves, bums and no-accounts—it's starting to get to me. I feel like a piece of metal on an assembly line and a lot of machines are pressing to make sure I turn out like every other piece of metal in the place. The guys say I'll get used to it and I guess I will, but I don't want to. They keep telling me you've got to cooperate, you've got to go along with "the man" (that's the hacks, the guards). They tell you when to stand and where to stand; when to eat, where to eat, and what to eat; when to sleep and where to sleep—they even tell you how to sleep, you know, with your head to the front of the cell so they can see it every hour. I feel like I'm being made into a robot or something.

PASTOR: Sounds like the Army—pretty rigid, eh? I guess it's tough to be much of an individual in a prison.

BILL: I'll say. Yesterday I missed the count. Good Lord, the guard went through the ceiling. About every three hours they count us— every guy in the institution. A few minutes before 11:00 A.M. I went to the bathroom—and believe me that's a word not even used here. They count at 11:00 and our shop total is 84 men. The officer counted 74, and he had sent 9 men out on passes. That totaled 83. Well, they found me in three minutes. The guard called me a sneaky worm. He says to me, "What's a matter buddy boy, you too important to show up for the count? We count at 11:00, you know, pal. The next one's at 2:00. You be the first one here, see? If I catch you goofing around again I'm going to bust you (write up a report), get it? How'd you like to lose about 30 days of good time, pal, and keep

us all company an extra month? Stupid cons, always pulling something cute."

Comment: If the pastor could follow up this talk by meeting with
the prison chaplain, he would get important perspective. He might
have felt indignant that a guard would humiliate a man (and the
stories of indignities reach many extremes). The central point in this
conversation, however, is the "changing" Bill experiences.

The first and most difficult adjustment of the new prisoner is to
face a routine of life in which his every move is observed with
suspicion and regulated with rigidity. "The count" is the central
ritual of the prison life. It takes place five to eight times a day. It is a
symbol of the inevitable cleavage between the watchers and the
watched—the guards and the inmates. As a ritual it becomes second
nature, but as a symbol it points to the most basic fact of prison
existence: a man is accountable every moment to the State. The loss
of freedom itself can be endured for a time. But such restraint is
rarely isolated from a far more destructive deprivation: *the man in
prison is never trusted.* Around the prison a high wall visibly
separates him from free society. Around the inmate a second wall
invisibly isolates him from all officials.

This is one reason that prompts us to say that the worst thing
about most prisons is not that a man loses his freedom, but that he
loses his dignity. It is unlikely he had much self-respect when he
entered, but prison life drives him further toward a degraded view of
himself that the return to freedom can hardly improve. No single
human experience makes more violent war on a person's self-respect
than prison life. We do not say that prisoners are "nice people" who
deserve better. We do not say they are innocent of violating the law.
We do not say they are just unfortunate victims of circumstance. We
simply assert that a brute fact of prison life is that it fosters a climate
in which dignity is lost. And this climate is the worst enemy of the
rehabilitative process. Whatever the church or the pastor does to communicate continued faith in a prisoner is crucial to his recovery.

The following month. The Second Visit:
BILL: Good to see you again, Mr. Roberts. It was great of you to bring
Marge and the kids up to visit. I hear you're going to take a little tour
of the place while I'm talking to my family.

PASTOR: Yes, the chaplain arranged it. I'm eager to see some of the things you've been telling me about. How's the new job coming, Bill?

BILL: A lot better. I never thought they'd make a salesman into a clerk but they're really hard up for men who can type. I was pretty rusty but I'm shaping up well enough. It's something to do. We work about five hours a day.

PASTOR: Five hours. That's an awfully short day. Doesn't sound like the best habit to get into, Bill.

BILL: Well, I'm lucky really. Some of these guys aren't busy for two hours a day. On my cellblock they've assigned twelve porters. These men mop down the whole place every morning—it takes them maybe 45 minutes. And that's it! Maybe the officer will send one down with the count sheet. Maybe a bunk gets broken and two of them will carry it over to the shop. Most of the time they just play cards and read magazines.

PASTOR: Can't they study or something? What about the school?

BILL: They could sign up for classes. Some of the men go to the A. A. meeting for an hour on Wednesdays. But most of them make a lot of excuses. They don't like inmate instructors and the books are all written in and pages torn out. The classes are dull. I suppose when you boil it down, they just aren't interested in bettering themselves.

PASTOR: Your job isn't that monotonous, then? Does it help you feel you're doing something worthwhile?

BILL: Naw. You know me, pastor. I've got to be selling something to enjoy the job. I like to sell myself to a customer and from there on, it's a snap to make him think he can't get along without the product. Guess I wasn't born to do much sitting down or standing still.

PASTOR: You like it best, then, when you're getting someone to believe in you.

BILL: Right—maybe that's why I feel so stifled in here. I mean, like last Sunday, right in Church (I've been going and trying to understand it)—well, right during the silent prayer I had this tremendous urge to jump up and tell them all off, every one of them, maybe smash somebody. During that silent prayer my mind was cluttered with the garbage I hear all day long—constant talk of rigged juries, crooked cops, bum raps, lousy guards, sex perverts in the shop, ways to get dope on the outside, the perfect crime, guys who pimp even for their own wives. Pastor, I'm losing track of what's normal and what isn't.

PASTOR: You mentioned perverts—is there much of such stuff?

BILL: Pastor, it is so revolting I don't even want to discuss it. Believe me, everything in the book, and plenty that isn't, goes on here. I'm starting to think the whole world is a cesspool. Do you think I'm cracking up?

Comment: It is often said, "Prisons teach poor criminals to be good ones." Bill Stone is fighting against the lessons his peers offer by the hour. A subculture does exist and it is very powerful. The cleavage between inmate and guards produces a code in which prisoners are often afraid to be friendly with anyone "on the other side." Some inmates will crash this barrier if exposed to a sensitive and concerned official. When this happens the stage is set for a therapeutic relationship. But here is the problem: one solid and honest relationship between an inmate and a staff member can hardly exert a stronger influence than the total atmosphere of the prison. It's like finding a towel to dry off with while one is standing in the rain.

Thus the lines between the real world and the worlds of fantasy, persecution, hatred and self-pity created by the inmate culture become increasingly hard to discern. Things like shaking hands, saying "good morning" or "thank you" drop out of sight. To put a hand on another man's shoulder is to risk the label of "homosexual." Prison life allows for no privacy. All mail is read, visitors are seen through screens, showers are taken in groups, toilets about the institution are without doors to allow for inspection.

In the atmosphere of constant surveillance, distrust and denial that pervades the prison world men find it very hard to trust themselves or to practice openness or honesty. Two grim realities are constantly at work in the prison: too few relationships with positive, healthy people and too much exposure to people who are negative and unhealthy.

A pastor who visits with prisoners can offer two direct suggestions. First, that the man in prison keep himself as busy as possible. Reading, writing, music, exercise, hobbies and study are indispensable resources for the man who is "doing time." Solitary activities especially, are essential. Cardplaying and competitive sports demand a careful choice of friends because prison is close living and inmate conflicts are not easy to resolve.

Secondly, to survive prison an inmate must maintain communication with the outside world. Mail and visits, newspapers and magazines are vital links with persons and places an inmate dare not lose track of. Mail, especially, is fresh air in a locked vault.

One month later. The Third Visit:

BILL: Pastor, I'm awfully glad you came. I suppose you know what happened.

PASTOR: Marge told me you had a bad week.

BILL: Listen, Reverend Roberts—you've been close to us through all this. And I'm terribly grateful. I think you know us pretty well—the good stuff and the bad stuff. Have you noticed any changes in Marge lately?

PASTOR: I can't say that I have, Bill. But apparently you've felt some yourself.

BILL: I know I have. I know Marge like a book. She's giving up on me. Her letter last week—she's got to get the kids ready 'cause school starts next month so she can't make it up to visit. I'm up here rotting away and she can't find a day to come see me. I know what's happening; I can feel it. That's why I wrote her and told her so.

PASTOR: What did you tell her, Bill?

BILL: Well, it goes back about twelve years—something we've never talked about. Before we were married she was in love with this other fellow. We all went to the same school. They were planning to get married. He got drafted and went off to the Army. I was passed up because of my eyes. I stole her away from him. He didn't write for a couple of months and she was lonely and I saw a good chance to move in. I swept her off her feet—you know, gave her the big rush: flowers every week, lots of parties and dinners and—we got married the day after I proposed. Well, I've always felt she still carries a big torch for this guy. He lives in town too—doing real well. He's married but I hear they aren't happy. They've got no kids. Mr. Roberts, I can just feel it in my bones. She's seeing him. She's seeing him—I know it. Our whole married life I've been second to this guy. Now she's got her chance. Nobody would blame her. I'm a convict, a loser.

PASTOR: Say, you're way ahead of me. Let's back up a bit. I hear you saying you stole your wife from a guy you can't measure up to. Have you felt this way all through your marriage, Bill . . .?

BILL: Well, I suppose so . . . Reverend, can you check on this fellow for me?

Comment: Bill has had a quarrel with his wife. The alert pastor will not be lead into playing detective to reassure a man that his wife is faithful. The real issue for Bill during his pastor's visit was that for his whole marriage he has apparently felt "second-best." Such a feeling may have pulled him far enough apart from his family to drive him to his thefts as a way of proving himself, and purchasing his wife's attention. At any rate, if the wife *is* growing apart from Bill, the pastor can only hope he has a good enough relationship with her that she will talk it over on her own when they next meet. He can pay her a call. He can ask how she is doing.

Extreme living conditions produce extreme reactions. Men develop a haunting suspicion that issues from daily exposure to a sordid, unhappy inmate population. Of course, institutional paranoia is not simply a matter of the imagination. Wives do give up and send "Dear John" letters, or divorce papers. Married prisoners worry about their wives' faithfulness. Every day they hear stories from men who have lived with someone else's wife. Their wife misses a visit, writes a hurried letter, or a nasty paragraph, and the inmate's fears are triggered into panic. He feels completely distrusted in the prison, so he begins to distrust those at home. Degraded daily, he imagines the worst of his wife and his friends. Humiliated often, he will burst out unpredictably in accusations of his church or his pastor for not caring. Such extreme reactions cannot be understood unless the pastor develops some sense of the process the inmate is undergoing.

A month later. The fourth visit: Bill has been punished by solitary confinement.

PASTOR: Hello Bill. It's good to see you.

BILL: Well, I'm sure sorry about what happened. It was a nightmare. No wonder they call it "the hole."* I was in there for three days—no books, no people, no bed—nothing but four naked walls. I nearly went nuts. I couldn't tell if it was day or night. After the first day, I started to sing songs just to hear somebody's voice. That's too much time even for thinking things out.

---

* Segregation, or solitary confinement—a form of punishment which isolates the man from everyone and everything.

PASTOR: I guess you had to think a lot just to keep your wits. Did you come up with anything?

BILL: Well, at first I was just plain mad. This thing about Marge has been eating at me. And I started to hate these guards. They act so damn superior. The staff is always right, regardless. The inmate is always wrong, by definition. Well, this time I knew my boss was wrong and I told him. I really told him. Then they took me into the deputy warden's office and that stupid clown asked if I would like to run the whole prison industry. I told him "No, thanks, I'd get too proud thinking I never could make a mistake." That wasn't the best thing to say, but I'd had enough. I was sick of eating dirt. I was sick of being second-rate. Hacks with third grade educations bossing me around like they owned me. They do own me, too. They say we've got some rights you know, but they are impossible to defend. I've had enough though. I learned I don't want to go back to "the hole"—ever. And I lost 60 days of my "good time" besides. It will take me a whole year to earn those days back.

Comment: The pastor can be easily misled in this situation. He can play lawyer and judge—trying to decide who was right, the inmate or the prison officials. This is futile. He can take the inmate's side entirely and run in indignation to the warden, commissioner of correction, congressman or governor. But his counseling opportunity lies in the probability that this disciplinary incident is a microcosm of Stone's inability to deal with frustration in a manner that is not self-destructive. Granted, he may have a boss too insecure to acknowledge error. Granted, the officials questioning him might be sarcastic, even intimidating. Granted, every single complaint of having to "eat dirt" and being made to feel second-rate might be grounded in actual ugly experiences. Nevertheless, in the midst of this is the unspoken, unrealized problem that Bill Stone is a person who *invites* such experiences. No doubt he has all his life. What he endures and what he feels are both dramatically exposed in the exaggerated setting of the prison world. The pastor's job is to help Bill see a connection between the anger, resentment and feeling of persecution which triggered the present incident, and similar feelings aroused by incidents which occurred when he was free. The emotional attitudes which are causing him trouble now are the very ones which set the scene for his crime and arrest.

On the other hand, prison discipline has its weaknesses. The rigid structure in prison is both good and bad. The good lies in the fact that so many inmates have had no sound discipline; they find their lives quite unmanageable. They need external controls. The bad is that most prisons use discipline entirely to keep order. The prison can break men down without much trouble and force them to accept the rules and make no trouble. The prisons can fashion most of the population into "excellent" (which means, "cooperative") inmates. The problem, of course, is how they will later make the transition from enforced discipline to self-discipline. For instance, men go to Alcoholics Anonymous meetings because they are told they are alcoholics. But there are no temptations in prison because there is no alcohol. The question is, when they are released will they freely join Alcoholics Anonymous, and can they continue to avoid the bar?

What we see in Bill Stone is the institution demanding he control his impulses. He is very tense over his wife and he hates authority. So he tells his boss off and gets in trouble. But the lesson he receives is offered in such a hostile and repressive atmosphere that it is unrealistic to expect him to internalize it. That's why many say that prison life isn't really reforming, it's conforming. Hence, resentments deepen. The prison rarely enlists men's earnest interest in changing, so prisoners find it necessary to repress their real feelings—both the positive ones and the negative ones. As Bill told his pastor, he probably will not tell his prison boss he is wrong ever again. The cost is too high. He will check his anger, mask his frustration, and become falsely polite to the officers and solicitous to the staff. But underneath, he will find it harder and harder to know what he is really feeling—unless, somehow, his wife, his friends, his pastor and maybe some people in the church can keep his personality alive by making him feel he's really a part of some people who love him.

Still, we must be realistic. Bill won't find much encouragement in prison. He is at a crossroads, and the encounter described in the above pastoral visit is a crucial one. Either he will soon take on the look of the institutionalized prisoner and join the inmate culture of men who hate the society, the law, the police and all who subjugate them; or he'll hitch himself to a mooring beyond the walls and stop fighting everyone. Some counseling is practically essential. Such dynamics are too deep to be experienced as Bill walks the yard or stares out his cell window.

A Summary

This chapter depicts four hypothetical pastoral visits. In the first visit Bill struggled with the unbridgeable barrier between himself and the prison personnel. In the second visit he struggled against absorption in the climate of anger and despair inevitable in the prison subculture.

The last two conversations reflect the inevitable tension between a man in prison and his family at home. In the third visit Bill hints at an overriding insecurity he has felt during the whole twelve years of his marriage. In the fourth visit his anger finally breaks into the open and he recapitulates under the prison microscope the kind of "acting out" that on a larger, more destructive scale precipitated his arrest.

The dilemmas these discussions uncover touch several critical areas. First is the importance of the pastor being able to discern the inmate's problems. In the first talk, for example, the problem is not that all prison guards are sadistic bullies, even though such incidents do occur. The problem is the inherent tension built into the daily contact between the keepers and the kept. If Bill is unable to accept it, and the pastor does not understand it, both will remain bewildered as the pastoral relationship develops.

A second issue the conversation typifies is the crying need for those in prison to have opportunity to work through the feelings prison life prompts and exposes. If, during and after the disciplinary incident mentioned in the fourth conversation, Bill *and* the prison officials could only examine the things that precipitated the outburst with Bill's boss, both parties could learn a great deal. But tragically, discipline in prison is entirely a matter of custody and control. Such crises could present the chance for insight; but not if the prison insists "We're right and you're wrong," and stops there.

Finally, the talks reveal a vicious cycle of antagonism between inmates and officials which is aggravated by the psychopathy of the inmate culture. If only this cycle could be broken by exposing the prisoner more to his family and to the free world the suffocating atmosphere of the prison might be dispelled.

These are some of the issues that will recur in later chapters as we search for ways and means for pastors and parishes to be ambassadors of Christ to those in prison. Our purpose here is to offer a glimpse of the prison world. A pastor cannot hope to understand a man in prison until he has some appreciation of the setting in which the prisoner exists. Bribery, homosexuality, cruelty, loneliness and other sordid sides of the prison world are vividly described in every novel about prison life. The worst thing about prison is not that a man loses his freedom. Indeed, confinement often rescues persons whose lives are hopelessly out of control. Nor does the worst of prison lay in its hardships and deprivations. Present-day prisons are incomparably more humane than those of previous centuries. Our fundamental point in this chapter is this: the worst thing about prison is the gradual eating away of a person's self-esteem. His dignity—often precarious to begin with—gets ravaged both by the climate of his peers and by the distrust that security measures breed. Hence it becomes extremely difficult for a person who enters a prison with disturbances not to undergo a widening of his disturbance and a deepening of his resentment toward society.

CHAPTER FIVE

The PASTOR And PRISONER

What To Do And How To Do It

All through the history of punishment runs the curious fact that practically the only people displaying a genuine interest in the criminals' lot are those driven by the spirit of a religious mission.

—James V. Bennett
Former Director, Federal Bureau
of Prisons

The pastor represents the church as it reaches over the wall into the life of an inmate. To bridge the gap he must know not only what to do, but how to do it. Instinctively, he knows what to do—write, send nurturing materials (bulletins, devotional booklets, etc.) and visit. Unexpected problems arise in accomplishing each of these pastoral goals, and it will help immensely to anticipate them.

When visiting, writing, and representing the church, the pastor must keep in mind (although we oversimplify) that the majority of prisoners have two preoccupations: their case and their family. A prisoner may be working to get a better cell, change jobs, find a friend, make the prison ball team, or compose a great poem. But the concrete questions he will most often pose for the pastor's understanding will be "How can I get out?" and "What will be waiting for me when I do?"

About Visits

The prisoner's need for outside contact is greatest at the beginning of his confinement. He is stunned and bewildered by a totally new environment. Several days pass before an inmate is cleared for letters and visitors. All prisons welcome contact between a prisoner and his minister; but pastors tend to forget that prisons are necessarily rigid institutions. Unlike a hospital, one cannot drop in at any hour. Careful advance preparations must be made within the context of the institutional rules. Every single correspondent and visitor must be approved by the prison.

Approval procedures vary widely, but in general the prisoner should request to see his pastor and secure prison approval for him to visit. It is good for the pastor to take the initiative by writing to the inmate, indicating interest in a visit. A copy of the letter might go to the chaplain. A letter from the institution is then sent granting permission for the pastor to write or visit.

Most institutions require proof of identity, especially if they do not fingerprint the clergy. Church stationery with the pastor's name on the letterhead will generally suffice. Sometimes further proof will be requested. The precaution is wise because prisons must strive to supervise and control a prisoner's contacts. Old cronies (disguised as clergymen) and old girl friends (posing as lady evangelists) are always testing the system, trying to gain undetected entrance.

The first visit. The first visit to a prison may be uncomfortable. You cannot be helpful when you feel uncomfortable, and you put the church in a poor light to the prisoner if he recognizes your uneasiness.

One way of avoiding the initial awkwardness is to make your first visit with the prisoner's family. You can propose to accompany them on a regular visiting day and spend the first visit with the family present. You might let them visit alone initially while you ask to meet the chaplain. You can return later for a private talk. But first, get your bearings so you can feel confident and act natural.

To make the first visit go smoothly, you need to know the do's and don'ts of prison visitation. If you notify the chaplain of your pending visit, he will give you helpful first-hand instruction. Rules, of course, vary from institution to institution, but the following suggestions may prove helpful:

1. Make sure you bring positive identification.
2. Don't plan to give anything *directly* to the prisoner. You might, for instance, consider it appropriate to hand the man a Bible during the visit. You can't. A dozen other people in the

visiting room would demand that they also be allowed to present gifts directly.

3. Channel Bibles, devotional material, religious medals, etc. through the chaplain. He must set the standards (size, value, appropriateness) for such gifts.

4. Don't send expensive gifts. A two-dollar hardbound Bible is better than a ten-dollar leather-bound Bible. (Some prisoner may steal the ten-dollar Bible to make a watchband with the leather.)

5. Keep your appointments. No single event, except the parole board meeting, excites as much anticipation as a visit. If you write and say you'll be there Wednesday—be there. If an emergency comes up at the last minute, call the chaplain, so the prisoner understands your absence. This is doubly important if you are bringing a member of the man's family with you.

6. Traveling any distance alone with the prisoner's wife can lead to misunderstanding. It's hard to realize the insecurities prison brings out in a marriage. Try to bring more than one member of the family with you, if possible.

Some prison regulations may seem strange and unreasonably rigid. Some are, but most of them are not. Here are three seemingly innocent short conversations which might take place in the visiting room:

1. "Reverend, I was wondering if I could ask a little favor of you. You see, there's this friend that I haven't heard from since I've been here. I've tried to write and my counselor sent out some papers but I've heard nothin'. If I can't get in touch with *her* I don't know what's going to happen. We were thinkin' about getting married before I got into this trouble. Here's the address where she lives. I wonder if you would write a letter to her for me?"

2. "Reverend, I'm taking some courses in the school here, but they don't have the books I need to study for it. I was wondering if you could get them for me? Here are the names of the ones I want. (Titles on a piece of paper reveal the books desired concern law, psychology, narcotics, or, perhaps, religion.) I'll pay you for them if you will get them for me. I can get my mother to send you the money."

3. "Reverend, I have a letter here to my wife. I'd like her to get it as soon as possible. It'll take a couple of days to go out through the institution mail and besides, you know, they read everything before it

goes out." With a knowing grin he continues, "Once in a while a man likes to say something to his wife that he doesn't want everyone reading, you know. I don't have a stamp, but would you drop this in the mail for me this afternoon? I sure will appreciate it if you do."

Or consider this letter to a pastor:

4. "Reverend, I have something that's been bothering me. I would like to talk with you privately for a while if you could come out and see me. I've tried to talk with these people here but I just can't seem to. They don't understand me or something. The chaplain here won't see me." (Or, "The chaplain here doesn't preach The Gospel," or "The chaplain is prejudiced against people like us.")

None of the above requests seems unreasonable and, indeed, they may not be; but *they are all very risky.* Consider some of the possibilities. In (1), the inmate is not asking the pastor to "take out" or "bring in" anything concrete. He wants to communicate with a female "friend." The pastor does not know who this "friend" is. She may be *just a friend,* but then she also may be somebody else's wife, or a former co-worker in crime. He gives the impression that every honest effort has been made to establish communication with her. He says "I've tried to write . . ." but he does not say why his writing came to a halt. He says "My counselor sent out papers," but he does not say for what purpose they were sent, or why they did not result in correspondence approval. The possibility of the pastor becoming a party to unauthorized and illicit communication is strong in this case, and only time would tell if serious implications would result. If the pastor complies with the first simple request, he may be hooked.

Example (2) may be the inmate's need to have something done for him, but it might also be a request to get unauthorized books into the institution. Example (3) points to the kind of situation where the inmate's approach combines urgency, implied violation of private rights by the institution's staff, and the solicitation for the pastor to put his sympathies on the "right side" of things. If the pastor grants this request, in many instances he will have violated state or Federal laws regarding traffic with prisoners. He is then actually subject to fine or imprisonment, or both. If his violation is not discovered he has placed himself in a position where he is at the mercy of the inmate for further demands—perhaps even blackmail.

The inmate who seeks special additional attention is illustrated in example (4). This type of inmate is a regular visitor to the office of many staff members. He has a hundred complaints and considers himself the victim of a thousand injustices. He always approaches with the implication that you and you alone can help him with his problem.

How do you deal with such requests? An indignant "No" can damage a relationship. But to get manipulated into compliance also has its dangers. For one thing it confirms a popular prison notion that a pastor is a pushover. Also, men in prison have tremendous needs to test authority, to maneuver around "the system." When pastors take part in this game it nourishes the prisoner's neurosis. He gains your sympathy first, your cooperation second, and your reputation in a crack third. The rules may not always be ideal, but helping a man break them is not the solution.

Be frank with the prisoner—tell him you are going to discuss his request with the chaplain and seek his guidance. If the request is legitimate, the prisoner will welcome the assistance of the chaplain, if it *isn't* he will urge you *not* to talk to the chaplain. You should see this as a red flag: you are being used, and perhaps misused.

About Mail

One cannot exaggerate the influence and value of mail in the life of the prisoner. Visits, of course, are more personal, but less frequent. Mail is the daily bread of a prisoner. A man cut off from all outside contact is a man in trouble. He becomes withdrawn. He is ripe for serious mental disturbance. He develops no resources for his release.

Among the inmate's immediate concerns on entering the prison is gaining approval of correspondents. The two major restrictions are of correspondents who have a criminal record, and female correspondents other than mother, wife, daughter or sister. If the prisoner is unmarried he may be permitted contact with a girl friend or common law wife.*

* In general the regulation of a prisoner's female contacts is designed to discourage relationships that might impair another person's marriage or create unhappiness in his own. In reality this censorship creates a stupendous detective task for prison officials because the inmates try all kinds of deceits to be in touch with those who have an interest in them.

Most pastors are not able to visit the prison regularly, but it is certainly possible to write regularly—or perhaps send your church newsletter. Be sure that church mailings are appropriate. A man in prison cannot respond to a plea for a pledge, and it offends him to receive it. It is asking for water from a stone.*

Writing is important, but exactly what you write is even more important. Many chaplains are obligated to censure letters to and from clergymen. The following are excerpts from letters pastors have sent to their parishioners. They offer a few examples of what *not* to write:

You should be ashamed of yourself . . . look what you have done to your family.

I saw your boy at Sunday school . . . he had tears in his eyes and the other children were teasing him because of you.

The church board met last night and your name has been removed from the church roll. Make a man out of yourself and you can come back. We don't want thieves in our church.

Your mother was in church as usual. Maybe your actions will cause your father to see his failings and come to church for a change.

Such remarks in letters do not help much. Chances are the recipient will not go to chapel for a month thereafter. In prison the wounds are raw. A letter of salt does little to help a man see Christ. More often it drives him further than ever from the church.

Be aware of contraband. If your congregation wants to send a package, be sure to request a list of what is allowed. Every prison is on guard against contraband, meaning *whatever is strictly forbidden inside a prison*. Contraband varies from institution to institution. In a typical maximum security prison, the following items would likely fall into the contraband category: pocket knives, cigarette lighters (require lighter fluid), gum (a dozen sticky uses, like filling a keyhole), shaving lotion (alcohol), allergy inhalers (drugs), expensive jewelry (encourages fights), money (though money orders may be sent to go into a man's account), glue (sniffing), and many more.

---

* Prisoners may earn five cents a day on the job! One of the very top jobs might pay as much as sixty cents a day. Wages vary from state to state but the vast majority of men in prisons earn less than thirty cents a day. The law requires them to save half of it (50 percent) for their release.

The Sacraments in Prison

Every prison chaplain serves communion to his congregation. Its gifts of repentance and forgiveness have deep significance to the man in prison—but the service is nondenominational. Private communion, administered in the familiar liturgy of one's own faith at the hands of one's own pastor is a special blessing. Sometimes a man's whole family can receive the elements with him.

Here again, there are obstacles. Finding a place conducive to communion is usually difficult. And it is against the law to bring alcoholic beverages (communion wine may be so classified) into a penal institution. So, even if it is not your custom, plan on grape juice. Such a pastoral service can be a wonderful means of grace, but it takes careful planning. You must coordinate it with the chaplain as he is your link to good arrangements. Some institutions cannot properly supervise it; others can.

Baptism is also complicated. Men who are converted in prison are frequently without a pastor. Baptism means most if it is not only entrance into the faith, but union with a church, a fellowship. In prison this is difficult. If your community is near a penal institution, you may want to say to the chaplain, "If you have a Methodist (or Lutheran, Baptist, etc.) who is prepared for baptism, we'll register him in our fellowship, and sponsor him until he is released." Or, the Chaplain may call you to ask if you and your congregation would sponsor a person newly committed to the Lord.

Death in the Prisoner's Family

Death is a frequent visitor to relatives of those in prison. In larger institutions hardly a week passes that a chaplain does not share with three or four inmates news of the death of a relative.

If there is death in the immediate family, feel free to contact the chaplain (by telegram or telephone), give him all the details, and ask him to break the news for the family.

Many institutions permit an inmate to visit the hospital or home in cases of terminal illness. If, for instance, a parent is critically ill and wants to see his/her son, have the attending physician notify the prison and verify the seriousness of the illness. One of the pastor's most important tasks at such times is to make certain such a visit is truly desired by the dying person. Sometimes another relative will insist on a "critical illness" visit without recognizing its hardship on the sick person.

If the death is in the immediate family most prisons will allow a funeral visit.* Usually the prisoner is accompanied by two officers.

Pastors deal regularly in the realm of grief. A pastoral letter to a prisoner who has lost a relative can greatly strengthen the relationship between the pastor and prisoner. On the prison side, a chaplain can have the prisoner read the appropriate Psalms and passages of the New Testament at the hour of the funeral to help him express his sorrow and direct himself to God.

Some men in prison show no emotion at the news of the death of a relative. For some this is honest because their ties with home are the thinnest of threads. To others, the news of death brings strong feelings of guilt. Mothers who die while their sons are in prison trigger an especially painful regret. Whatever a pastor can do to assure a prisoner that the church has embraced his family during their grief is of invaluable comfort to him.

Your Denomination and the Prison

Although prison chaplains must function on an interfaith basis, they understand the unique value of a denominational ministry and are glad to cooperate with interested denominations.

Some denominations designate a pastor who has a parish in the vicinity of the institution to function as a contact pastor. This means, for example, that should a Baptist inmate wish to see a pastor of his own church, the chaplain can contact the Baptist clergyman that has been designated by his denomination. When denominations do not take responsibility for such appointments, their members are without denominational pastoral care.

When such a denominational mentor has been appointed, a pastor who lives many miles from the institution where his parishioner is confined can count on this fellow-pastor to stand in for him. Officially-

---

* Most states limit funeral visits to the same state. The Federal Government permits funeral trips over a wider area provided the inmate has a satisfactory prison record.

appointed contact pastors are a great assistance to the chaplain and the prisoner, as well as to the denomination and the home congregation.

State and local councils of churches should instruct denominations to appoint a contact pastor for each institution in the area. When a contact pastor has been officially appointed by the denomination, the other pastors of that denomination should recognize the authority placed in his hands. This does not mean that the home pastor shouldn't write or visit the prisoner; but it does mean the denomination has made arrangements with the institution for pastoral care of those who do not have a home church.

What to Avoid

About the records. Reports of all sorts are gathered on each person confined. Personal data on family conditions, psychological findings and legal matters are confidential and not available to the parish minister. Good professional standards require that the viewing of such documents be limited to the proper officials on the staff.

About evangelizing. Some clergymen view every prison as a concentration of outcast sinners. They feel the harvest is ripe and the laborers are few. They may wish to develop a ministry to others in the institution, who are not of their parish.

A chaplain's goal is to develop a broad religious program—suited to the varied needs of his prison "congregation." Every prison chaplain has felt indignation at fellow ministers who storm the institution so eager to save souls they disregard his religious program. When this happens clergymen should not be surprised at the chaplain's reluctance to permit them to do whatever they wish. Prisoners need every opportunity to hear about and respond to the Word of God. But penal institutions are abnormal places, and the benefit of every grace, including Salvation, must be geared to this reality. Therefore, every pastor who wants to help with worship, religious instruction, or counsel to prisoners should veiw the institution as he would a church—respecting the will and awaiting the invitation of its spiritual leader, the chaplain. Where there is no staff chaplain, pastors do best to work through the Council of Churches and the prison warden to develop a program related to the larger church.

CHAPTER SIX

The PRISON CHAPLAIN'S PROGRAM

Professionally-trained prison chaplains are largely a product of this century and the shape of the chaplaincy is undergoing significant change. Chaplains are in transition from the early days of being a lone voice on the prisoners' behalf, to being a member of a diverse rehabilitation team.

Initially, chaplains were often the only professional persons in the prisons. They served as legal advisors, athletic directors, marital counselors, release planners, educators, as well as leaders of worship. In the course of the past twenty years, however, all of these accessory functions have been taken over by specialists.

Despite the continuing evolvement and redefinition of the chaplain's role, certain pastoral functions remain vital and changeless.

1. He is a *minister* to his congregation. His duties include conducting worship services, administering sacraments, visiting the sick and the segregated, counseling the distressed, and teaching the Bible. At times he will minister to the prison officials, who, in a less defined and more informal sense, are also members of his parish.

2. He is a member of the penal institution staff, which may call for making reports to the parole board, sponsoring inmate groups such as Alcoholics Anonymous, interviewing all new men, or sitting on various decision-making committees.

3. He is a liason between the prison community and the church. In this capacity, he will be in contact with pastors of prisoners, preach or speak in churches and community groups, and encourage inmates to seek spiritual resources in their home church.

The Chaplain's Program

The correctional chaplain is active in the same areas as a parish minister. The difference lies in approach and content. The approach of the prison pastor is interdenominational. The content is geared to people caught in crisis. He constantly keeps these two distinctions in mind: he represents all Protestant denominations, *not* merely his own; and every person in his parish is in trouble—serious trouble.

The sacerdotal ministry. Worship services are held weekly, and more often during the holy seasons. Communion, baptisms, funerals, and, on rare occasions even weddings,* are sacred events over which the chaplain presides. In any and all of these services, he may function alone or invite a parish pastor to share in his ministry.

Persons who visit prison worship services are usually surprised at the reverence and seriousness of the prison congregation. Most services appear in every way typical, except that no offering is taken and the congregation is all the same sex. Anthems are sung by prison choirs (in some chapels, they even wear robes).

Interdenominational worship enriches the prison a great deal, but there are minor obstacles to be overcome, due to the variation in ritual and tradition among those participating. Flexibility is important. For instance, Protestant communion is usually served in the Chancel area, (Episcopalian, Methodist, Lutheran style) at an altar rail. The worshippers are invited to receive the elements in the manner closest to their own tradition. They may stand, sit, or kneel; they may be given the bread, or they may take it in their hand. The uniformity of the Mass makes such adaptations unnecessary for the Roman Catholic Chaplain.

Many institutions have interfaith chapels. All three groups— Protestant, Catholic and Jewish share the same sanctuary. A revolving chancel stage displays the basic symbols of each religion. The nave itself is free of symbols. Such "close living" in worship demands a cooperation and respect that is beneficial to all three groups.

There are other points where faiths overlap. Regularly the chaplain is called upon to handle letters from home containing news of

* Regulations regarding marriage vary, and in some prisons marriages are not permitted.

death, divorce, or serious illness in a prisoner's family. If the inmate is Catholic, and a priest is not available, it may fall to the Protestant Chaplain to convey the message. At such times, religious lines are erased and prayer becomes a common language that transcends doctrine.

Jokes are often told of the prison chaplain's "captive congregation." In most institutions, (excluding youth institutions), however, chapel worship is a voluntary matter. The percentage of attendance will vary a great deal, but usually prisoners who worship regularly are a minority in the institution. A chaplain reaches those who are seeking, those who want to be reached. Bribes such as "chapel attendance will help you toward parole" are a misuse of religion. The important thing is that those stamped with a sense of guilt, those caught in the agony of doubt, those searching for comfort or direction or a new life, may find the Word of God read and explained, the inspiration of hymns, and the power of prayer readily available.

The teaching ministry. Bible studies, lenten services, baptismal instruction and confirmation classes are common tools of a prison ministry. Bible correspondence courses play a prominent role in the teaching ministry. A religious library is useful too. Inmates, on the whole, do more reading than the average person, and religious literature is widely circulated in prisons.

The broad and basic Christian doctrines are a part of the chaplain's instruction. Prisoners readily identify with biblical characters:

Adam and Eve	The problems of temptation, sin, men and women.
Cain and Abel	Sibling rivalry—murder.
Moses and Pharoah	Living in captivity.
David and Bathsheba	Infidelity (by a good guy).
Jesus and Judas	Betrayal (by a friend).

Jesus' arrest, trial, execution: a world inmates know well. The Reverend Carl Burke, a county jail chaplain, has done a splendid job of taking biblical material and, with the help of his prisoners, translating them into the vernacular of the offender. Note the gripping impact of his prisoners' (largely youth) version of the 23rd Psalm.

The Lord Is Like My Probation Officer*

The Lord is like my Probation Officer,
    He will help me,
        He tries to help me make it every day.
        He makes me play it cool
        And feel good inside of me.

He shows me the right path
    So I'll have a good record
    And he'll have one too.

Because I trust him,
    And that ain't easy,
        I don't worry too much about
            What's going to happen
                Just knowing he cares about
                    Me helps me.

He makes sure I have my food
    And that Mom fixes it.
    He helps her stay sober
        And that makes me feel good
        All over.

He's a good man, I think
    And he is kind;
        And these things will stay
        With me.

And when I'm kind and good
    Then I know the Lord
    Is with me like my Probation Officer.

Teaching in prison must also be centered in ethics. Distorted views
of morality are the bread and butter on which many prisoners were
raised. An example: "Do unto others, *before* they do it unto you."

* Carl F. Burke, *God Is for Real, Man* (New York: Association Press,
1966), page 39.

The counseling ministry.   Many chaplains consider the counseling ministry the most important part of their work. Prisoners are constantly in crisis. Their lives cry out with tragedy and trouble. Relationships of deep influence are almost essential in the chaplain's ministry.

No chaplain goes through a week without being forced to realize that the term "father figure" is not just psychological jargon. Prisoners need counsel, and they seek it. By and large they are dependent people. They may approach the chaplain with a strange mixture of motives, but they do approach him. The following are samplings of frequent concern:

1. FAMILY RELATIONSHIPS: "I've no word from my wife—would you write her? She's either sick or deserted me. She mentioned divorce in her last letter."

2. FINDING A JOB: "Do you know anywhere I can get a job? I can't be paroled without one and I've made 184 applications and not a nibble."

3. FACING GUILT: "These people here don't understand me. I'm no criminal. This is all a horrible mistake. I was just riding in the car. I had nothing to do with the robbery."

4. SUDDEN RELIGIOUS CONVERSION: "Can I have a Bible? I've decided to go into the ministry. What do I have to do to get ordained?"

5. CONFLICT WITH OTHER INMATES OR WITH STAFF: "I work in the hospital. I'm in trouble. Some guys are pressuring me to steal pills for them. I'm afraid I'm going to get busted up."

Many more could be listed. Sometimes the initial problem becomes the focus for helping the inmate. Many times the "presenting problem" is a feeler for the inmate to determine whether he can share deeper concerns about himself.

The following letter illustrates a number of points discussed thus far. It is an actual letter that passed through a chaplain's office for his approval. It was written by a "very religious" inmate who is taking Bible courses, writing to a minister, and preparing himself for the ministry. He describes his conversion, his need for help from the church and his reason for entering the ministry in a single letter.

Dear Reverend Cotton:
I greet you in the name of Jesus Christ and I praise God for the victory. I have won the victory of Christ through the free Bible course from

your institution—it has revealed God's word to me in direct revelation! He has given me the knowledge and strength to complete the enclosed lessons and I eagerly await His Divine guidance on the next ones.

I am in prison, serving a four-year term on burglary. I was raised in a Christian home—my whole family were Ministers of the Gospel of Jesus Christ. When I married, I was not yet saved. My wife was very religious and wanted me to become a minister but I continued to drink and carouse and keep bad company. Satan had singled me out and had led me away from the glorious path of salvation in Jesus Christ.

I was mad at my wife for trying to help me and I beat her for seven years, whenever I was drunk. We were separated and I really went to town then—and Satan thought that he had finished me when I wound up here in prison.

But I had a vision. Christ appeared to me and told me that my wife was going to be married to a preacher. I wrote to her and found that it was true. She had divorced me—although I had not received the papers when I found this out through direct revelation. But I also found that the man had walked out on her before the wedding.

I now know what the true path that Christ has laid for me is. My wife had wanted to marry a preacher and I would not be one before. The dream-revelation was God's way of showing me what the true path for me is. This is why I am sending these lessons back to you so fast and I look forward to receiving the next ones soon.

Yours in Christ,
    Signed . . .

This inmate presents himself as a model prisoner, who has seen the error of his ways, found Christ, and is a changed person bearing all the fruits of his newness of life. In fact, he is not. He is deeply disturbed. He constantly manipulates the authorities, reveals strong hostility toward any who do not see religion his way, and has little awareness of his many angry and obnoxious patterns of behavior. He has found in religion a mask to hide his self-centered and destructive ways. He has found a new approach to regain his wife, and he has used religious prophecy to reassure himself and others that the plan of God insures the reunion of his family. He presents his own pastor and the prison chaplain with the toughest possible challenge. He is not asking for guidance or self-understanding. His unrealistic picture of the world and himself is rigidly fixed and he will hear only those voices that reinforce his illusions.

In contrast, other men approach the chaplain or their pastor with enough anxiety and uncertainty about themselves that they are "open" to new insight. By way of contrast, consider another actual letter written to a chaplain by way of a request for an interview:

Dear Reverend,

Since age nine I have been in and out of some type of punitive institution. When just a child (I cannot recall what my first arrest was for) I was sent to an institution just outside of my home in Pennsylvania. From the moment I set foot in the place, I had to fight for everything from keeping a "cookie" we used to get once a week, to keeping the older boys from using my body for whatever perversion might strike their fancy. It was while in this place, I learned how to really lie, cheat, steal and all the other things, that are relative to deception. Still a child (I think I was fifteen, when I smoked my first reefer) I made a sham of going to school. One day I discovered that nothing would happen if I stopped school altogether. I found I had a talent for waiting tables: people liked me, I was unassuming, I did what I was told and was quick to learn. I left home. Wandered to New York, (where I worked some) Asbury Park and Atlantic City. Always seeking out older people, always looking for an easier way out, always using what money I made, from an assortment of jobs, for drink, smoke and needless to say, heroin. Finally, at the age of twenty, I was arrested for using drugs. There has been the full gamut of arrests since then. It's the age old story, Sir, of not knowing, not caring, running loose, not knowing where I was going or why. I came all unprepared to the fork in the road and before I could realize the folly, I had galloped too far to turn back, or better, I did not know how to turn back.

I have tried to give some picture of what my life has been, up til now. If any one thing could be blamed for the mess I made of my life, surely I would have to bear the full brunt of it. This September, I will reach my 33rd birthday and all I have to show for three decades of living is a long yellow sheet. I have made a full cycle. In a very real sense, this place is just like my first reformatory, only on a bigger scale. But there is a profound difference and this is really what the gist of this letter is all about. For the first time in coming in and out of these places, I realize that I have been going from cycle to life-wasted cycle. What little I have ever had, I have managed to lose. My parents have nothing to do with me, my wife is not sure she wants to take another gamble with me, and but for the Grace of Almighty God, it's a wonder I have not lost my mind. I am not a hardened criminal, hopelessly beyond all possibility of change. I feel close scrutiny of my record will bear that out. I have been my own biggest problem. Heroin and liquor have only added bitterness to an already anguished life. How is it, that I realize all of this now? Because this is the first time I have ever tried to realize it. I am daily taking stock of myself, thinking of hope, wondering if there is any left in the world. When I look at myself, I see a man I have never seen before and what I see, Sir, frightens me. I want a chance to overcome this fright. I do not want to be just another lifeless man, forced to fit into a huge regimented machine. I want a chance to become a useful citizen. Whatever it takes, probation, parole, whatever demands society might make, I want a chance to meet them and I want to do so as a man, who is seeing himself for the very first time.

Thank you, Sir, for your time. I know the real test must be made outside and lots of times, when someone feels he is ready, readiness is in fact a long way off. I have heard you speak and I respect your way of reaching people. Any advice or guidance you may have in helping me find what I seek, I look forward to, and I hope you will talk with me.
I am respectfully,
        Signed . . .

The difference between these two men (represented by their letters) is that the first one uses religion to mask his problems; while the second finds in religion the opportunity to discover what some of his problems are. The second man does not even know the four Gospels. But he is closer to Salvation than he realizes.

Pastoral Visitation in the Prison

A chaplain needs to see the men where they are so that he knows (and they know he knows) where and how they are living. In his appointed rounds the chaplain goes to the hospital (or infirmary). He goes to the segregation units (often known as "the box" or "the hole") where men are sent for various reasons: discipline (the prison within the prison); protection (someone is threatening him); observation (disturbed or perhaps psychotic inmates); isolation (initial quarantine and orientation).

But he should also make an effort to stroll through industry, watch a ball game, wander the yard—because he alone in the institution has access to all quarters without being suspect as one snooping for trouble. Of course, he must be careful. If he becomes too closely identified with the prisoners, and avoids the custodial force, his work is impaired. It's a thin line. "Whose side are you on" is an unconscious question constantly influencing both the keepers and the kept. Chaplains must act so their answer to the hidden question is "I am on neither side and care about both sides."

The Chaplain's Congregation

J. Edgar Hoover's famed remark, "A boy who goes to Sunday School, doesn't go to prison" simply does not stand up. Many prisoners know the Bible far better than the average congregant. By and large, those in prisons do a great deal of religious searching. They often are very hostile to the church but not to the Bible, and not to the job of making sense out of life. The prison chaplain finds (and this holds true for all forms of the institutional ministry) his people are serious and searching: "He who is well has no need of a physician." Chaplains rarely complain of apathy in their congregation.

Chaplains see that a good deal of soul-searching goes on within the man in prison. He tries to work out his relationship with God, with others, and mostly, the inner relations with himself. Often, he is unable to separate the laws of God and the laws of man. Too often, since he cannot feel forgiveness from man, he feels there is no forgiveness from God. He may deliberately develop this reaction because he does not want to deal directly with God. He wants others to deal with God for him. He prefers that others accept responsibility not only for his religion but for everything else that has value or meaning.

The Chaplain, The Pastor, and the Prison Ministry

There are many points in a chaplain's program where a fellow clergyman can be very helpful. These "points of contact" will naturally vary with the type of institution and the goals of its chaplain.

To be honest, chaplains sometimes label the pastor as one who "knows nothing of the raw facts of life." And parish ministers often eye chaplains as strange ducks who have "left the church." Until we get over that kind of nonsense and admit that there are diversities of gifts and ministry, the work of Christ is mocked. Wherever the parish ministry and the prison chaplaincy choose to join hands, the following checklist for cooperation may prove helpful:

1. Special services of worship—sacred days, evangelistic services, etc., are excellent occasions for visiting clergyman.*

2. Administering communion—to those of one's own denomination (and to families).

3. Visitation and correspondence.

4. Pastoral counseling and instruction to inmates.

5. Gifts: Magazines for men in the prison hospital

Altar appointments to enhance the prison chapel

Funds for chaplain's discretionary use

Greeting cards for inmates to send home on birthdays, anniversaries, etc.

6. The Ministerial Association—to evaluate the church's responsibility to local penal institutions.

To consider issues of penology such as capital punishment, release-work programs, parole programs.

To foster community understanding and support of prison programs.

7. Helping with a prisoner's release planning—his job, living situation and church.**

8. Care of the prisoner's family.

If You Want to Be a Prison Chaplain

Approximately 250 chaplains are now working in state and Federal prisons. As in every part of the church's work, standards are becoming more important, and specialized training is mandatory.

Standards for chaplains. The Federal Bureau of Prisons has established criteria for chaplains, as does each separate state. Councils of Churches have played an important role in setting standards and

* One of the correctional chaplain's greatest friends, incidentally, is the Salvation Army. When no one else will help, the Army can always be counted on to care and to work for a man or a cause. Salvation Army has special divisions for ministry to male and female correctional institutions.

** The matter of planning for release is of such importance, we have given a full chapter (X) to its consideration. The same is true for the inmate's family (see Chapter VII).

recruiting qualified clergymen. Standards vary from state to state, and from state to Federal service but the following credentials are usually required:

a. College and theological training.

b. Ordination in a recognized denomination.

c. Approval of good standing with man's own denomination.

d. Experience in a local parish (2–5 years).

e. Clinical pastoral eduction (2 quarters or more).

f. Nomination by a representative personnel committee—of local or State or National Council of Churches.

g. Approval of officials (warden, superintendent, commissioner) of penal institution.

We may expect an increase in the role and value of the Council of Churches as it sets standards, stresses specialized training, screens candidates, and requires reports of chaplains serving in institutional ministries.

Organizing a New Penal Chaplaincy

No single influence has been more important to the changing institutional ministry than clinical pastoral education. It has been the conference table for talks between religion and medicine; religion and psychiatry; religion and penology. Any clergyman interested in serving a correctional institution should view clinical pastoral education as essential preparation for such work

Ministerial associations or local councils of churches wishing to establish a chaplaincy program in a city or county jail, a juvenile court, or a family court should take these steps:

1. Consult with the Council of Churches* on state and national level for guidelines and standards.

2. Consult with a chaplain supervisor (a chaplain accredited to conduct programs of clinical pastoral education for guidance in the institutional ministry).

3. Develop a working relationship with the institutional officials and involve them in the personnel committee and chaplaincy program planning.

* The National Council of Churches of Christ, 475 Riverside Drive, New York, New York.

CHAPTER SEVEN

NETWORKS Of SUFFERING

For every person inside a prison, there are four persons in the free world directly affected. It is these four persons who can benefit most from a church that cares. The church can do far more, in direct ways, for a prisoner's family than for the prisoner himself.

We turn attention to those at home by offering an actual letter from an inmate's wife to a newspaper editor after her husband is gone:

I still find it hard to accept, for all around me his presence is felt. His belongings are still as he left them. I kept telling myself it wasn't so— they haven't taken him away—but the day arrives when it must finally be faced and accepted. This day is either the making or breaking of a woman. She must decide if she will stand by him, and help in every way she can to make his time as bearable as possible, and show him beyond a doubt the strength of her love, or she can turn on him and abandon him to face his confine-life alone. She finds that, all too suddenly, she must face the ways of the world alone. . . .

True, I am not confined, nor my freedom restricted in any way, but my hours and days and weeks and months are spent very much alone, for the children—even as much as they mean to me—can never fill the gap left by my husband's absence. My world revolves around my husband's letters, and our all-too-short visits. I live only for these. The very hardest part of my time is when the children ask 'Why doesn't daddy come home anymore?' I can feel my eyes filling with tears of heartbreak as I search for words to try to make them understand. I know that I must be stronger than I have ever been. I try to be patient and understanding with my husband, for I know the anguish and worry he suffers thinking of his loved ones. I can only reassure him that all is well, and that we still love him, for he needs us now more than anything else.

I wait, and live and pray for the day when I can walk through the prison gates, arm-in-arm with my husband, for we must face what the world holds for us together, and as one.

From a waiting wife,
(*Reprinted from a prison publication*)

When society isolates an offender from its midst, he is not the only one who pays a penalty. What happens to families when the father goes to prison? In general, the prisoner's family feels three areas of distress:

1. The family's financial support.
2. The family's relationship to the community.
3. The family's relationship to the father.

In general, this chapter suggests the ways responsibility for help in these areas lies with the Government (for area 1); the Christian laymen (area 2); and the pastor (area 3).

The Family Finances

Every prisoner is the responsibility of the Government. Welfare assistance is the chief means by which the Government provides for problem number one—food, shelter and clothing for a family without an income. Every state has a Welfare Department which will supply a pastor with the qualifications necessary to apply for welfare aid and the amount of money available. Standards vary from state to state. Benefits vary according to the size of the family, age of the children, type of housing and resources of the family. Social workers interview the family and evaluate its individual needs. Surprisingly, some wives have little conception of the resources open to them through the Welfare Department. Some families would not consider accepting welfare. Often, a mother goes to work and is unaware that even though she is working, many states have minimum standards that would qualify her for welfare assistance to supplement her earned income. The pastor may call the Welfare Department in his area to learn precisely the assistance available. The amounts will vary by state, area, size of a family, age of children, etc.

A pastor who has a good relationship with a family can inquire frankly about their finances. Can the woman go to work? Would her working be the best solution to the financial problem? Has she called the Welfare Department and learned the resources available to her through the Government? Are there lawyer's fees that should be reduced or spread out by time payments? Is there indebtedness—car or house payments that cannot be met? The pastor may be in a position to ask a lawyer or accountant in the church to advise the wife gratis. Are there any chores, such as maintenance of the house, that can be taken on voluntarily by church members to reduce her expenses? These are questions the alert pastor can raise with the family and with their close relatives to face candidly the plain facts of survival when the bottom falls out of the family's income structure.

One footnote about family finances is offered to keep the picture in perspective. Wardens and parole boards often receive letters from wives that tell them bluntly, "Please keep my husband in prison as long as the law allows. Things have never been so good. We are not rich, but at least we can count on something. When he comes home, we go off welfare. He'll make a decent wage but most of it will go for liquor (or gambling, or narcotics). We are better off without him, so please don't send him back."

Such rejection goes deeper than the financial unreliability of a husband. This is the kind of cleavage that needs evaluation and honest probing. In some situations, divorce may be the most realistic course of action. She may be thinking about it and afraid to say so. Help her voice these feelings openly. Be sure the couple takes plenty of time to think through a move so drastic and painful. Encourage them to talk about it together so if divorce seems inevitable, they gain some understanding of the reason their marriage failed, and some insights into what lies ahead.

The Family and the Community

What can the church do through its laymen?

The State can, and does, make provision for a family that has lost its financial support. The State cannot do the same for a family's dignity and acceptance in the community. The church can—through its pastor and through its people. The pastor is the liason between a humiliated, broken family and the people of God, the Body of Christ. His role is to help knit that family tightly into the life of the church so that they will know that even though father is away and times are bad, they belong more than ever to the family of God.

That is good theology! The Church ministers to those in need. But to translate theology into flesh and blood requires knowledge and planning. Each pastor works his own way. You may consider selecting one or two strong couples in the church and asking them to function as "sponsors." Perhaps two of the deacons can take this on. However a pastor goes about it, he needs to find and counsel the persons who are to stick close to the prisoner's family. Here are some suggestions about what "sponsors" can do:

1. Arrange rides for her to visit the prison. Child care may be needed while she is gone. If the prison is near, she will want to take the children. It is good for children to see their father—even in a prison visiting room.

2. See that the children have a male figure close by: an uncle, a grandfather, an elder in the church. Help them find some man to look up to, to be with, to learn from.

3. Check that the children have groups where there are concerned men accessible: Boy Scouts, athletics, the band, the youth group at the church. There are many possibilities for the children to be in service groups and peer groups.

4. See that the wife has social opportunities. Someone can pick the family up for church picnics. Ladies can ask her to help cook at church dinners. Don't wait for her to show interest. She may be reticent or self-conscious. You may have to open the door and walk through with her the first few times.

5. Raise added money if the family needs it. See that the youth group mows the lawn if there are no older children. Oversee her home's maintenance.

6. If the family has pre-schoolers, arrange for them to be in the church's day nursery. If your church does not have one, call the church on the next corner. Take extra measures to see that the child is admitted, because his needs are greater.

7. Send the prisoner packages: cigarettes, toiletries, fruit. (Check Chapter Five for the rules regarding acceptable gifts.) It shows others are thinking of him as well as his family.

By and large, the above tasks are best done by concerned lay people. Few pastors have the time for such close attention, and such work is tangible expression of Christian concern. If a pastor can interest some of his people in such work, he is training his people to practice their faith. The pastor will need to consult and advise the sponsors but not to do their job for them.

At the same time, there is pastoral work the minister can do with a family. It has mainly to do with the third area of a family's needs, namely:

The Family's Relationship to the Prisoner

What can the church do through its pastor?

First, there is the question of whether a marriage is solid enough to survive imprisonment. If a man gets a ten to fifteen year sentence, it will be at least six and a half years before there is any possibility of family reunion. Length of sentence is a factor that must be discussed. Sometimes an offender's crime is an unconscious effort to escape marriage and parenthood. If this is the case, the husband and wife need to look closely at whether their marriage can be continued. It is quite impossible to generalize about the question of divorce while a man is in prison. Our only point is that the pastor should not simply assume it is the couple's duty to stay together no matter how bad things were before prison, or how long they will be separated, or how many children they have. Nor is the question of divorce a matter that can always be resolved at the start of a man's incarceration. Feelings change and decisions need to be made accordingly.

Closely related to the future of a prisoner's marriage is the question of the children. What should they be told about their father? Their age, of course, is a big factor. For younger children who cannot comprehend the judicial process, two things are important. First, whenever tension strikes a home and somebody goes away, the child's instinctive fear is "Did I cause this to happen?" Children have many strong feelings toward their parents; and to the child's mind, it is awesome to imagine they might have the power actually to destroy a parent. Parents are tense during such crisis, and they have less to give the children. It becomes easy for the child to imagine that "Whatever is going on, I'm to blame."

The mother, the pastor, and others need to be as honest with the child as possible: that times are bad now but they will get better; that father has to go away because he has broken the law. And it is just as important to say to the children, both collectively and individually,

"This is not your fault. Daddy still loves us but he must go away and we will visit him because we still love him." None of these thoughts will stop the children's endless questions of "Why?" or "How come?" You can explain the law and prison and then they will promptly ask, "Why was daddy bad?" The point is to reassure them, in the midst of unanswerable questions, that *they* are not to blame, that they are still loved by mother and father, and that the family is different now and they must accept it.

The other question involving children is the issue of visitation. Some parents will be repelled at the thought of their children entering a prison. The pastor can give invaluable help by assuring the parents that their fear and their embarrassment is natural, but the children will feel neither. In every visiting room, other children will be present. If a family is to survive the trauma of prison, the children need to write and visit their father as often as possible. The visits will destroy any wild fantasies that daddy is dead or lost forever. It will keep alive their awareness of him as a person—a face, a voice, a man who cares for and about them, and will someday return.

Every prison chaplain interviews hundreds of men who are frantic about their family's well-being. A letter that is stiff and guarded, a missed visit, no mail for weeks, are all signals that something is wrong at home. With too much time on their hands, men think of the worst possibilities. So many wives and mothers are reluctant to tell the man in prison when things are bad. They want to protect him. A child is seriously ill. A relative dies. The loan company is threatening to take the furniture. A son is failing in school. So often these are matters families withhold in the name of pity. In general, this is neither wise nor helpful. It makes letters stiff and visits stilted. The person in prison is usually very sensitive. He isn't fooled. Something is wrong and he can sense it. Pastors can counsel families to write regularly and share everything—even the worst. The truth is, it is good for a man in prison to know and share the burdens of his family—even though he may feel helpless to do anything but pray. If the marriage is to stay alive, it must be fed partially on common tears, enduring the "sickness, want and sorrow" of their wedding vows. It will not be easy for the prisoner to learn how difficult things are at home but it will be realistic. Through letters, he may very well get his first genuine picture of his family's problems and feelings. If he can't cope with them in writing, he'll do no better after release, when he must face them in person.

These are concrete ways a church and its pastor can minister to a man's family in his absence. Families that hold together through the crisis of incarceration are different afterwards. They have withstood humiliation. They have known genuine confession of sin and forgiveness for failure. Any congregation and pastor who takes an active hand in sharing their burdens presents Jesus Christ to those Jesus loved much.

There are two other situations that present special problems in pastoral care and require a different kind of help. The first is the common-law wife.

The Common-Law Wife

Many men go to prison and leave behind a trail of women and children to whom they are not legally bound. Most states recognize relationships in which a man and woman have lived together as husband and wife for a reasonable period (usually at least a year) as "common-law marriages." Where such situations exist (and they are very common among offenders), the pastor has a special problem in pastoral care. He is dealing with a problem that is far more complex and important than this brief section indicates. It is one of a cluster of social ills woven into the pattern of criminality. Such issues plague and bewilder social agencies, which realize the children are innocent victims, and prime candidates for social maladjustment. It is unfair to blame the church for every social ill and to ask the church to resolve all social problems. But it is not unreasonable to cry out that the leaders in local churches must recognize that a host of people live illegally and irresponsibly in a myriad of family relations, leaving a sordid, tragic trail of children to try and find God and love in a godless, loveless vacuum. So often people ask, "Why, when a marriage fails, do persons simply leave, or enter into a common-law marriage? Why don't they get a divorce and remarry legally?" The main reason is that it costs money to get a divorce. The poor are preoccupied with shoes and cereal and can't afford the legal costs of divorce. Divorce is a luxury only the affluent can afford.

The Single Prisoner

Many, many prisoners are unmarried. Many have no one who continues to care except their mother. This is a different family problem. It is risky to generalize, but we find many in prison whose criminal actions represent triumph over their parents, and emancipation from parental tyranny. The pastor must evaluate the individual family situation.

Mothers often feel a strong resentment they cannot admit. They ask themselves, "What have I done to deserve this? How could he bring me such grief?" Or, if they are quite unable to face the reality of a son's actions, they may claim with certainty their son was "framed." Or, if they are more honest, they may be asking, "What have I done or not done that has led to this?"

Whatever the particular problems of the parents, several questions might occur to the pastor: "Has the prisoner been the scapegoat of a troubled family? Has he been dominated by his home? Is it good for the prisoner to return to this home and stay under its influence?" Sometimes it is: but very often it is not.

A prisoner's letters home often reflect a new-found objectivity. Many prisoners are in their twenties, and confinement brings their first awareness of an over-dependency on Mother. Here, the pastor needs to help parents see angry letters as a sign of health and strength. The prisoner may make his break from home in very hostile fashion—criticizing or condemning his parents. They will feel guilty and angry. The pastoral work here is much the same as helping parents of teen-agers endure adolescent defiance. They must recognize the struggle to be a person, to find independence that the prisoner, like an adolescent, is going through. Parents need help to redirect their interests and emotions to other areas and other people. It may be quite evident to a pastor that a young man went to prison partly because his parents would not let him grow up. But the minister cannot just watch them cripple themselves with guilt, or let the prisoner destroy them with condemnatory letters. Without inviting them to weep openly about their failure, he must point the way to places where they can succeed. Some people fail miserably with their own children, but are able to give to the children of others.

The Long-Range Picture

This chapter has focused the pastor's attention on the people in the community who crucially affect a prisoner's life: his wife (or common-law wife), his children, and his parents. It is worth re-emphasizing that this is the cluster of persons for whom the pastor and church can do the most. As you think through the possibilities and suggestions offered in this chapter, we offer one overriding principle. *Don't work alone with prisoners and their families.* Some pastors concentrate on confidentiality to the point of preventing their people from ministering to one another. You journey over to reach a prisoner who lives on the other side of a wide chasm. When you go over, be sure to build a bridge over the chasm for the prisoner and his family to come back and join the respectable. One way to build the bridge is to take along some mature laymen as you make the trip to the isolated family of the prisoner. These laymen will then become the bridge back into the community.

The prisoner and his family also need to feel accepted by society itself, "the good people." Prisoners feel there is a large word stamped on their forehead for life. The word is "GUILTY." You may not regard it so, but they do. All their lives they pay a "hidden debt" for violating criminal law. Therefore, all your work—writing, visiting, counseling, providing, etc.—is of little value if that family does not feel itself an integral part of an accepting group. Hence, behind all your work with the family of a prisoner should lay the long-range perspective that you are preparing both a home and a community for a crucial time of reunion with a prisoner.

CHAPTER EIGHT

YOUTH INSTITUTIONS

Persons under 18 years of age were identified as having been involved in 30 percent of the serious or Crime Index offenses which were cleared by arrest. The young age group, 10 to 17 years, now makes up approximately 15 percent of the total United States population and based on police solutions of crimes, they commit 42 percent of all property offenses. . . . The percentage increase in the involvement of these young persons, as measured by police arrests, is more than triple their percentage increase in the national population.*

If a man goes to prison at age 25, chances are good he was a troubled lad at age 15. Society provides correctional institutions for adults who violate the law and for minors who violate the law. But there are two crucial differences:

1. The law and the courts are directed toward rescuing children who are victims of intolerable parents and unhealthy surroundings. Unlike the criminal courts, juvenile courts are less dominated by the goal of proving guilt and issuing punitive judgment.

2. When a young person breaks the law, there are many options other than incarceration. Parents, clergymen and judges can find ways to help the youth before his behavior demands that he be confined to prison. Our purpose in this chapter is twofold:

1. To define types (or levels) of juvenile delinquency and clarify the options open for a youth who violates the law.

2. To discuss the special opportunity of the church to uncover trouble early and help families take initiative to head off later disaster.

* FBI *Uniform Crime Reports—1965*, p. 20.

What Delinquency Means

The term "juvenile delinquency" refers to illegal behavior on the part of minors. In most states, a minor is a youth under age 16.* There are various degrees of seriousness to delinquency; and accordingly, the court plays various roles. At one time, its role may be primarily guidance to the parents. In other instances, it may use the law to reinforce parental supervision. In still another case, it may have to remove the child from his parents, either to protect the child or the society. Whatever the court does, its aim is primarily remedial in contrast to the punitive orientation that dominates adult courts.

Thus, the pastor must guard against viewing all delinquency behavior the same. Chronic truancy from school is against the law. Yet it could reflect a sick mother confined at home, rather than a boy who is out of control. Stealing is against the law but it is important to know whether the child is angry at the world, is following the gang, or is starving. Parents, pastor, child welfare agencies and the courts must be flexible and cooperative if they are to find the *cause* of the youth's delinquent behavior and work together to prevent delinquency from solidifying into criminality.

Suppose a 13-year-old boy is caught setting fires to his parent's property. He has violated the law and he comes before a juvenile court (or a family court or domestic court). His behavior may be viewed as emotional disturbance and the court may recommend counseling. The procedure would likely begin with a diagnostic evaluation in a psychiatric setting for at least ten days. In addition to the treatment plans such observation affords, the court is interested in a basic issue: is the boy safe to himself and to society? If the court does not see a danger of violence in the youth, it may begin by requiring professional treatment, on an out-patient basis in preference to an institution. We will review types of out-patient and in-patient facilities shortly. The point here is that in spite of the fact that a child has committed an act of delinquency (in this instance, arson), the judge can use wide discretion in deciding:

—whether to adjudicate the behavior "delinquent" or not;
—whether to define the behavior as a violation of the law, or as a symptom of emotional disturbance;

* The Federal Government defines a minor as under age 22.

—whether to remove the child from the parents, or to allow him to remain in his home while he gets treatment.

A second approach to a delinquency problem is exemplified by a family that recognizes the child is beyond their control. Suppose a boy develops a pattern of truancy from school and is stealing things from home. Such delinquency sooner or later would bring the boy into the courts. If parents get in touch with a family service agency or child welfare bureau they can find help before they face a courtroom. The child welfare agency will then begin an evaluation and can, with the parent's consent, refer the child to a private institution. Few parents can afford the cost of a private institution, but if they go to the Welfare Department, it will assume most of the expense of institutionalization. This course of action also allows the parents, instead of the court, to maintain custody of the child.

Yet this is a difficult move for a parent because the youth can easily interpret the placement as punishment and complete rejection by his parents. It is easier for parents to let the court be the punitive force. A clergyman who recognizes parents are simply unable to supervise their child does a real service by helping them approach a social agency (family service, child welfare, etc.) before the court is *forced* to confine him in a government institution. A good private institution or school will generally have a better program and staff than the state facilities.

Finally, state institutions exist so that the court is able to confine minors whose behavior is illegal and whose record indicates other measures at control have failed. States have various names for such institutions including Reform School, Industrial School, Training School, and Youth Development Center. In most of these institutions, the youth is confined for a prescribed period of time (a sentence) and his confinement becomes part of his legal record. This may limit his future in terms of military service, employment opportunities and holding public office.

When a young person gets into trouble, he is saying clearly to the adult world: "The world inside me is in an uproar and I cannot control it." His behavior represents an "acting out" of inner rage and desperation. Young people get through the growing process only with the support, guidance and controls offered by the people about them.

When such controls are weak or absent, their life gets out of hand. Their inner conflicts are great, their inner controls are undeveloped, and the surrounding support and restraint is inadequate. They get into trouble. The pastor should recognize that, by law, a minor is not entirely responsible for himself. When the law is violated, the question arises, "Who has and can exercise adequate responsibility for the child?"

1. We look first to the parents or foster parents. Suppose they are weak, or ill, or separated, or disinterested so that they cannot effectively help the youth develop character and controls?

2. We look then for adequate parent substitutes like an aunt and uncle, a concerned family, foster parents, whose care can be reinforced by the school and the church. Suppose such efforts fail and the youth gets more out of hand?

3. We look next to the court (a juvenile court, family court or domestic relations court). The judge or justice of the peace then has two options:

    (a) To return the youth to the community, refer him to a counselor and make him regularly accountable to the court (through a probation officer); or

    (b) To remove him from his natural community and sentence him to an institution where the controls and the supervision are greater.

A pastor may become involved at any one of these three levels—with the parents, the parental substitutes, or the court. At whatever point he enters the picture, he must keep in mind the basic fact that in dealing with youth, some adult must take responsibility. Each crisis or incident of delinquency raises this problem: who can adequately handle the young person's urgent need for support and controls? As the question of responsibility appears, the pastor can play a vital role. Part of his work is to search out the resources available for helping the youth find an acceptable relationship with his world. Let us review some of these resources briefly. Out-patient care and residential care form the two main categories.

1. Out-Patient Care—where the child continues to live at home with parents, foster parents, relatives or friends.

2. Residential Care—where the child is lifted out of a natural community and placed in a more controlled setting.

Types of Out-Patient Services

Usually out-patient care is the starting point unless the child is dangerous or his environment is so disturbed that any benefit available through treatment will be canceled out by his family setting. The forms of out-patient care include:

1. Professional counseling on a private basis with a psychiatrist, psychologist, social worker, minister, guidance counselor or family physician.
2. Professional counseling through an agency such as a child guidance clinic, family service association, a pastoral counseling center, or regular contact with the bureau of child welfare.
3. Counseling through an agency of the court, such as regular contact with a probation officer.

The agencies and professional resources vary widely from community to community. Pastors who know the agencies of his area and develop working relationships with them can be of inestimable value in helping families get to the right place—both in terms of their child's needs and the family budget—and get there *in time.*

Types of Residential Care

When delinquent activity cannot be averted with the child remaining in the family, he needs to be removed (temporarily at least) from the family. But even at this point, the child need not be under court jurisdiction and need not have the stigma of a record. Families that can not adequately supervise their children can still act responsibly by approaching the child welfare agency and enlisting their help in placing the child in a private or church-related institution.

Where the parents do not act before a child's behavior reaches the court's attention, the juvenile court must take responsibility. The judge has at his disposal all of the options open to the parents—outpatient treatment, private residential care—plus, if he has broken the law, the authority to sentence a youth to a correctional institution.

Institutions can be described as "open" or "closed." An open institution is a minimum security facility where the youth experiences community living—school, recreation, chores, competition, and sometimes counseling—under the supervision of trained adults. The living group is usually a cottage, and the cottage has "house-parents" who live with the children. In general, an open institution is without walls or bars so that controls are based on verbal restraint and a well planned program. From time to time there are runaways, but usually they pose no danger to a community. A closed institution, on the other hand, is one with tight security. The youths are under constant supervision and are far more limited in making decisions for themselves. It is generally some kind of reform school with locked units under the surveillance of a guard rather than a cottage parent. It is, in essence, a prison for youth who need maximum security. Most youth institutions fall somewhere between these two atmospheres, with degrees of freedom permitted *after* a youth has accepted the limitations required. Sometimes an institution maintains both open and closed facilities with young people "graduating" by cottages as they are able to cope with increasing freedom and responsibility.

Pastoral Guidance to Families of Juvenile Delinquents

A decision as important as institutionalization should not be made without professional consultation. This may come from a diagnostic study in an out-patient facility. Suppose a minister is worried about a young person's constant unacceptable behavior. Suppose further, he is able to talk with the parents and they feel just as helpless and bewildered as he. They have tried counseling with a child psychologist but the youngster is not improving. He has been known to beat up other children, to break their toys, to skip school periodically and to steal petty things from dime stores. As yet, he has not been caught and the law courts are not yet involved. The parents may feel anxious at the thought of placing him in a private institution for boys. How could the pastor help them? He could recommend that the family go with the child to a diagnostic clinic and request a professional evaluation of the child and his family circumstances. If the clinic recommends institutional treatment, then the family and the pastor can feel assured and strengthened in the difficult decision to seek residential care.

But what if the clinic recommends an institution and the parents are unwilling to accept it? Then the pastor, with his own uncertainty clarified by experts, can take another avenue to help the child. First, he may try the child's school to see if they can persuade the parents to place the child. If they cannot, then the pastor and the school can approach the judge to call the family into court the moment a truancy or legal infraction gives the judge authority. In such cases, the pastor may not win any popularity contests with the youth or his family, but he may free the child from a family setting that is working increasing damage on the child's life. Most of the time, children who commit crimes are saying they need help. The crime is a symptom, a signal of distress. A child who steals food when there is food at home is saying that in some other way he is not being nurtured at home.

In Francis Frellick's excellent book, *Youth In Conflict*, the author emphasizes the tremendous challenge to the church to do preventive work with young people *before* the courts of law are forced to intercede. Those who work in correctional institutions so often examine a prisoner's record noting that he touched the edge of a church's life and never really took hold. Or they note his respect for a particular teacher or youth leader or minister, and wish that somehow, a long way back, someone could have responded to the prisoner's muffled call for help. We feel an urgency to call pastors' attention to the endless possibilities for the church taking a more active role in preventing children and youth from the downward cycle of trouble that leads toward a correctional facility.

Spotting Trouble Early

It can be done. The alert and trained person can evaluate a home where the child is in the first year of school and anticipate children who will later become delinquents. One reliable and skilled research team interviewed 1,000 families, following them over a ten-year period and calculating those who would become involved in delinquency and those who would not. Their predictions of young persons who would have delinquency problems and those who would not were 90 percent accurate.*

* A brief survey of this research project is contained in "A Manual of Procedures For Application of the Gleuck Prediction Table," New York City Youth Board, 79 Madison Avenue, New York, New York 10016.

What interests us are the five factors the researchers scaled after interviewing families.*

1. Discipline of boy by father.
2. Supervision of boy by mother.
3. Affection of father for boy.
4. Affection of mother for boy.
5. Cohesiveness of family.

Amid a number of conclusions drawn from this research effort, two seem very important to the church. First, it appears that the family is the central and decisive factor in juvenile delinquency. Second, it is clear that future delinquent behavior can be anticipated in very young children (age 5 or 6).

The church has a special advantage in that its program embraces the entire family. And pastors enjoy a special relationship with families since they continue to visit people in their home.

Of course, many troubled families are unrelated to the church. They present a challenge in outreach. But many troubled families *are* in the church. And our emphasis here is on the crucial importance for every church to study its program critically and at all levels— worship, Christian education, men's and women's associations, committees, etc.—in terms of how such efforts account for the needs of the family.

We feel strongly that churches should not be embarrassed at developing a strong active social program. Couple's clubs give Christian marriages the chance to be nurtured by other couples. Lively youth groups reach young people where their interests lie—helping boys and girls relate to each other and discover one another in wholesome and well-rounded activities. If a church has bowling teams and square dances; if its church school mixes boys and girls together; if it sponsors Scouting troups and Alcoholics Anonymous meetings; if it blends the recreational with the spiritual; if it offers both Bible study and theater parties, it then reflects that same appreciation for the unity of life that Our Lord demonstrated when he taught at wedding feasts and marketplaces as well as in the Temple. When the Gospel pervades each one of the many dimensions of life, there will be

---

* Later in the study, the Gluecks reduced their table to three factors, omitting factors 1 and 3 and proving the three scale predictive table just as reliable.

points at which the whole family and each individual member can feel welcome, loved and "at home" in the family of God.

Churches that separate the secular and the sacred, that believe temporal realities do not mix with spiritual realities, miss countless chances to touch broken lives and give children and youngsters strength that their parents cannot offer.

This book is directed toward the problems of persons in correctional institutions. But those who work in a correctional setting recognize the enormous responsibility of the pastor in the parish. So much preventive and remedial work is done in many parishes. The churches find one creative way after the next to help young people before an institution is required.

A church in California takes part in a program called "Friends on the Outside." They help the families of prisoners they do not even know: teaching home economics; providing extra clothing; helping mothers who get sick, and standing in readiness for various emergency services. Each summer lay people who work with "Friends on the Outside" recruit youth from the churches and develop a day camp program, offering children of prisoners recreation, crafts, snacks and, most important, attention and guidance from Christians who care.*

A pastor in New York City knew nothing about juvenile delinquency or crime. But his church was on the edge of a slum area and he wanted to make an effort to help its youth. He sought out the leader of a juvenile gang and his girl friend. He got them together with another young man and woman, both college freshmen and good athletes. The four of them took off for a weekend retreat. They planned out a busy summer designed to keep that neighborhood gang out of fights and trouble. They had "emergency" programs of swimming and dancing ready for the days when it was hottest and the youth most restless. They worked out contests, socials, picnics, and work projects—such as combining with the church's youth group to paint the local police station. They organized a special vacation church school using adolescents who had no identity with the church to help in the craft and recreation areas of the school. This required

* For information about this program, an outstanding volunteer organization for helping a prisoner's family, write "Friends on the Outside," 712 Elm Street, San Jose, California 95126.

advanced training meetings. That summer, four young people and a pastor helped reduce the street riots and avert trouble. Their efforts allowed youth from the church and the unchurched to meet and work together.

We cannot claim that these kinds of programs will cure juvenile delinquency, but we can be sure that help given at this stage in young people's lives, before a correctional institution is necessary, places the church at the center of a redemptive ministry.

Churchmen can find many places to assist in youth institutions—both private and state. The chaplain can be a valuable link for volunteer work. Sometimes a youth group "sponsors" a cottage—arranging picnics, sending birthday presents, leading singspirations. Laymen can offer volunteer tutoring or religious education, or assist in recreational programs. One of the most skillfully organized volunteer programs in the country is at The Childrens Village, New York.*

On the level of pastoral services, one of the most effective places for clergymen to work is the juvenile court. Ministerial associations or Councils of Churches should give serious thought to establishing a juvenile court chaplaincy program. Such a ministry is too specialized to utilize parish pastors on a rotation basis.

Clinical training programs are preparing clergymen to take up a ministry in the courthouse. They help families through the crisis of the courtroom, develop resources among the local churches, and counsel with troubled youth at the most critical moments of their life. They develop a consulting relationship with attorneys, judges, and the myriad of social agencies that are often bewildering to families and to pastors. They work with young people on probation from the courts. Juvenile court chaplaincies are one of the special opportunities for the church to present Christ and make a difference to families in trouble.

Should a Council of Churches wish to establish a juvenile court chaplaincy, it is important to select a committee to develop a job description of what the church could do in conjunction with the

---

* The authors have appreciated the helpful counsel of the Reverend James Tallman, Chaplain of The Children's Village, Dobbs Ferry, New York. Added guidance on specific projects for a church to aid a private youth institution may be obtained by writing to The Children's Village.

courts. Valuable guidance in developing a juvenile chaplaincy program and in interviewing qualified men can be obtained by writing the Department of Pastoral Services, National Council of Churches of Christ in the USA, 475 Riverside Avenue, New York, New York 10027.

CHAPTER NINE

ISSUES Of INTEREST

The obstacles to the rehabilitation of offenders are enormous. Sharp resistance comes from every corner of the society: from the courtroom, from the prison, from a vindictive public, from each human being's fears of his own aggression. Our purpose in this chapter is to first explore the public misunderstanding that obstructs progress in criminal law and then to examine a few of the obstructions in the legal process itself: the courtroom, the judge's chambers, the attorney's office, the jail, the jury, the parole board and capital punishment.

In the field of mental health, the past generation of Americans is slowly crawling out of superstitions about mental illness and realizing that personality diseases can be treated successfully. As people gradually realize that everyone must cope with some degree of mental disorder and that insanity is not a hopeless, incurable condition, they are able to help support the complex job of healing.

There is a parallel movement in penology—slower, more recalcitrant, and complicated severalfold by the long tradition that evil can be beaten out of people something like dust is beaten out of a blanket. As a society matures, it increasingly recognizes criminal behavior as a reflection of its own weaknesses. Seeing crime as a part of our own limitations, we can become less preoccupied with vindictive judgment, and more concerned about conditions which breed crime and programs which give offenders a chance to recover. Because the pastor's greatest exposure is not to those who go to prison, but to those who obey the law, half of this chapter deals with three familiar clichés that "lawful people" often believe. In these clichés we may find clues to the hidden social resistance to progress in better criminal justice:

1. Fit the punishment to the crime
2. Punishment deters criminal behavior
3. Crime does not pay.

Fit the Punishment to the Crime

Cliché number one.

This familiar slogan is a primary consideration in fixing sentences. It provides an interesting commentary on American values. Since money is among the chief gods of Americans, bank robbery usually carries a lengthy sentence. Because cars today are plentiful, auto theft is usually 1 to 5 years. Because many Americans are afraid of sexuality, sex offenders are the worst of criminal scum. Because tax evasion, embezzling and fraud (white collar crimes) are "sophisticated" forms of crime—involving indirect aggression—they require less retribution and such offenders avoid imprisonment with astonishing frequency.

The flaw in such time-honored guidelines is that a preoccupation with the crime itself overlooks the criminal. Many bank robberies are the impulsive, desperate acts of immature men under pressure—men who could be helped and restored to productive lives if they didn't have to count on thirteen years of time passing before they were eligible to see a parole board.

The alternative, of course, is to fit the punishment not to the crime, but to the person who commits it. This would require as much effort in measuring a man's troubles as measuring his guilt. The central obstacle to shifting our emphasis in sentencing criminals is human vindictiveness. The notion, for instance, that anyone who commits rape should be either killed or castrated is an unvoiced attitude that governs people more than we realize.

Students of human behavior have given attention to the history of retribution and vindictive judgment. One explanation that recurs in literature on this subject is that each of us has within himself criminal thoughts and fantasies which he sees expressed or "acted out" by offenders. In punishing such people, we gain an emotional relief, a kind of redemption from our own guilty feelings. Sacrificial lambs and scapegoats for expiation of sin is a practice well understood by clergymen. Behavioral scientists suggest that society must punish vindictively to relieve its own guilt. If this is correct we have a very concrete sign of a nation who has not yet understood or accepted the atonement of Jesus Christ. That same crowd that eagerly brought an adulteress before Jesus for his judgment before they stoned her has not yet heard or understood his searching reply, "Let him who is without sin cast the first stone."

Consider a contemporary situation. Suppose a youth strains for 22 years under the severe grip of very repressive, dominating parents. Suppose he yearns for some freedom from their oppression, sensing deep down that if they have their way, he will remain their little boy all his life. Suppose he cannot possibly admit to himself that he hates them for never offering him a modicum of freedom or trust. Suppose one hot night he sneaks off impulsively, gets drunk and takes a car. Suppose he meets a spunky 17-year-old girl who suggests they go for a ride, and the pair takes a wild, carefree, four-day drive to Mexico. What could happen to this young man? His fate cannot possibly be anticipated because there are too many contingencies. However, the possibilities are these:

1. He may be arraigned in a state court where he resides on charges of:
   (a) Grand Larceny—for the auto theft.
   (b) Corrupting the morals of a minor.
   (c) Assault—a charge that always accompanies a sex offense because touching the "victim" is involved.
   (d) Statutory Rape—which means sexual relations with a person under age; the question of her consent (or even seductiveness) is immaterial in sexual relations with a minor.
2. He can be arraigned a second time in a federal court on charges of:
   (a) Auto Theft (under the Dyer Law of transporting a stolen vehicle across a state line).
   (b) Kidnapping (on the possibility that the trip was against the girl's will).
   (c) White Slavery (taking a woman, regardless of her age, across a state line for purposes of prostitution).

This young man could be found guilty of one or all of the charges in both state and Federal courts and serve a sentence in:

1. A State Prison* ranging from:
   (a) Grand Larceny, Second Degree—up to 10 years.
   (b) Corrupting the morals of a minor—up to 3 years.
   (c) Assault, Second Degree—up to 5 years.
   (d) Statutory Rape—up to 10 years.

2. And following parole in the state prison, he could be transferred to a federal prison to serve a sentence for:
   (a) Kidnapping—10 years to death penalty.
   (b) Dyer Act—1 to 5 years.
   (c) White Slavery—1 to 10 years.

This is the enormous range of possibilities. What actually would occur would depend on many things. For example, it would depend on:

   —whether it happened in the city or the country. (By and large, the courts are much tougher in rural areas.)
   —whether his parents defend him or turn their backs to him.
   —whether he is white or another race.
   —whether he has money to pay a lawyer or has to accept a court-appointed attorney. Money works wonders in criminal cases.
   —whether the girl assumes some of the blame or turns on the boy.
   —whether the girl's parents seek to protect their daughter's reputation by placing all the fault on the boy.

This is a theoretical case, but such contingencies are quite real. The boy might go free on probation, or he might spend his whole life in prison. These are the "facts of life" in law courts. They represent the incredible unevenness and unpredictability of human justice.

The point is this: unless two important efforts are made, the sentence for these violations of the law will be misdirected. What must happen is:

One, that the energies and resources of the court be directed toward uncovering and understanding the particular problems of the particular person who stands accused, and

Two, that the community reaction—meaning the boy's parents,

* Sentencing laws vary from one state to another.

the girl's parents, the press and its readers—be held in check so that its indignation (or pity, or fear, or anger, or whatever the human reaction may be) does not make an impact upon the type and degree of punishment the boy is given.*

To expand these points further, consider first the problem of understanding the motivation for an offense. The reasons a person violates the law cannot be explained adequately under the pressure and tension of a courtroom. Many times the reasons are not clear to the offender himself. A crime needs to be seen not as a disease, but as a symptom of problems that lurk in the background of the offender.

The device for discovering such problems is a "pre-sentence investigation." Some courts do a thorough "pre-sentence investigation." *Many courts do not.* Without a professional evaluation of a person's family and the circumstances leading up to the crime, a judge is in an extremely difficult position for assessing the needs of the offender. As long as the courts continue to sentence without a pre-sentence investigation, the punishment will be measured out without knowing much more about the offender than the facts needed to determine his guilt.

The church's job in this regard rests on two fronts: social and individual. On the one level, society and legislators must be convinced that a court should function not only to judge who is guilty and who is not, but also to determine "why." This will require money, training and competence. After the question of guilt is established, and *before* judgment is pronounced, the question of "why" requires added study. The courts will not have such information without an extensive pre-sentence evaluation.

The second level of response—individual pastoral intervention—is even more basic to the task of the church. Behind the law's predominant attention to degrees of guilt and degrees of punishment lies the human problem of revenge. The law reflects the human conscience, so legislatures and judges and juries cannot be blamed because they

---

* It is important to emphasize that we are not suggesting that prisons are full of innocent youngsters. They are not. The vast majority of those in prison have records of several previous arrests without convictions. Few men in prison are there because they sang too loud in the choir. Our concern here is not over men who are not guilty; it is over sentences that measure the wrong problem.

are accurately mirroring human self-righteousness.* Thus, the important work for the church is to remind its people constantly that: "Vengeance is mine, saith the Lord. I will recompense."

Let us be clear that we are not saying punishment itself is un-Christian. Nevertheless, our task, as Christians and creatures of God, is to redirect our indignant, injured conscience away from punishments that merely measure our hurt, toward punishments that are measured to an offender's problem. This will not happen without legislation. And the legislation will not happen until Americans are made aware that the courts cannot exact justice that is righteous, while parents, citizens and most frequently the newspapers, pressure the courts to account for "public sentiment." Public sentiment is a fickle, immature arbiter. It can be influenced in alarming ways by the news media. The public is in no position to be objective or to know the facts. Pastors cannot easily stop the press from making headlines out of human tragedy. But they can apply the Gospel of Christ to the problem of human justice, and there is much to teach.

For example, one of the church's constant tasks is to explain the meaning of sin. Pastors know that murder is not an isolated sinful act; it is an ugly symptom—the product of human alienation from God and other men. The problem of Cain began not with Abel's death; but earlier, with a festering jealousy. Hence, it is never enough to announce the law, "Thou shalt not kill," and define the punishment. The law, Paul tells us, only acquaints us with our sin, our separation from God. It does not stop us from hating or from killing. What alters such evils is the personal discovery of God's love and human love. Unless we experience these we are unaware of the terror of our separation, and the infinite value of the human personality.

Thus, to punish each other, and mete out the punishment according to how evil we have been, is like shooting with our eyes closed. We do not look at the target. Similarly, to mete out sentences that register how *evil* the sin is actually ignores the nature of sin and makes punishment a matter of quantitative vindication. It focuses on

---

* One example is that attendance at executions is by invitation only and tickets are usually reserved for members of the family of the person or persons harmed by the one who is to be excuted. This is a curious way in which authorities take cognizance of a person's desire for vengeance.

the offense and not on the offender; it punishes the sin and ignores the sinner. When the Christ told us the Sabbath was made for man and not man for the Sabbath, his message was clear. Laws are designed to guide and restrain men.

Yet there are a host of people for whom "life is a rock, and the law a chisel with which they would carve it in their own likeness."[*] Our prison programs have made abundantly plain that a period of years— one, five, ten, twenty or forty—in which the rock of life is made much harder and less vulnerable frequently only makes the offender increase his determination to break the chisel. We release thousands of prisoners every year who are less equipped to live within the law than they were when they were confined. We are more sophisticated today than to demand an eye for an eye, but we continue to study in detail the unlawful act itself, and ignore the long-troubled personality that perpetrated it. The central Christian truth that declares God is more vitally concerned with persons than with laws has not yet made its meaning known in the courts of human justice.

Punishment Deters Criminals

Cliché number two.

The thought of prison horrifies and intimidates the vast majority of human kind. And for the vast majority, surely the possibility of imprisonment plays an important role in encouraging obedience to the law. In this sense, the old presumption that punishment deters criminal behavior is quite accurate. Yet there are those in society who are not threatened by the prospect of exposure or punishment. England once had a policy of publicly hanging pickpockets. Huge crowds would gather to witness the execution. As persons huddled together spellbound at the horror of the hanging, pickpockets moved deftly in their midst, lifting the wallets of those watching their comrades hang.

We can no longer take for granted that the threat of punishment, or punishment itself, prevents criminal activity. It is well said that the purpose of a lock on the door is to keep basically honest people from temptation. But locks do not keep thieves from breaking in. It is just

[*] Kahlil Gibran, *The Prophet* (New York: Alfred A. Knopf, Inc., 1923), p. 44.

as true that the threat of prison does not keep a large number of persons from violating the law. And since well over half of those who go to jail are released and return a second time, we can hardly claim that confinement itself deters those who violate the law.

To become acquainted with criminal pathology is to be impressed with the multiplicity of ways in which some people taunt others to punish them, and go to exciting lengths to make sure that they do. Punishment, then, is not necessarily a deterrent for persons who unconsciously need to be punished. It may prove satisfying to the victim of a mugging to know his attacker is spending two years in prison. But if the mugger is satisfied also, then it is only a matter of two years before he will return for a renewal of his masochistic reward.

How could a person possibly be "satisfied" by prison? Suppose he is trapped in a miserable marriage with six children he cannot support, and a boring job that he hates, and a sick mother who blames him for not providing her with a better doctor, and four "friends" pressing him to pay his gambling debt, and a bad case of a venereal disease. It might be quite satisfying (and rewarding) to be deprived of his freedom and "forced" to go to prison for a time. Furthermore, there was always the chance he might fleece a hundred dollars from his victim and not be caught. Then he would have "one more chance" to bet the races and see if he could "luck out" of his situation.

If the pulpits of our churches would ring out with the paradoxical message that crime really does pay (emotionally and financially) and that punishment as prisons administer it does not achieve one of its central purposes, namely, to correct improper behavior, things might begin to change. Of course, someone will quickly cry out, "But we must punish criminal acts. What else can we do?" Agreed, we must punish. Punishment is an essential ingredient of law and order. But there is punishment that humiliates and scars the human mind; and there is punishment that respects and enlarges it.

One example suggests how punishment can be directed to constructive ends. In Minnesota, a new method has been approved for men serving a short sentence. Suppose a man is given 90 days for drunkenness and assault. He may be required to do those 90 days on weekends only. He would have to work five days a week to support his family, and for almost a year (45 weekends) he would have to check into prison each Friday night and remain until Sunday night.

This is a form of punishment that does not let the man escape domestic responsibility, one which meets his needs not only to be punished, but also to have close supervision during his leisure hours. A second example of punitive measures that warn a man without ruining him is the use of a "short dose" for first offenders.

FAST DOSE OF PRISON
Short Stays Enough For 1st Offenders

Santa Fe, N.M. (AP)—A swift dose of bitter medicine is being tried in New Mexico's system of sentencing first-offenders convicted of crime.

District Court Judge Frank Zinn of Gallup is credited with developing the medicine, a taste of prison life.

Nearly four years ago, Judge Zinn sentenced a man to a one to 10 year term. He suspended all the term except for 29 days, which the man was ordered to spend in the penitentiary.

Only 12 Return

Since April 1, 1963, Prison Warden Harold Cox has received 124 persons ordered to serve short terms ranging from 30 days to six months, with the remainder of their sentences suspended. Of this group, only 12 —less than 10 per cent—have returned to prison.

Cox believes the 30-day term is the more effective, and he feels the program works more effectively on certain types of person.

The prisoner must be contrite and really want to improve, Cox said. Also, a first offender who is afraid—fearful of entering prison and fearful about his future—has a better chance of being rehabilitated, the warden said.

If a man is sent in for 30 days, he has not lost this fear of being in prison by the time he is released. But if he remains for six months, he tends to adapt himself to prison life.*

There are other possibilities,** but not without society reordering its philosophy of punishment to reduce vindictiveness and turn more attention to an offender's individual problems.

* Newark *News,* August 28, 1966.
** Other examples of efforts to "punish" men by increasing their sense of responsibility rather than completely depriving them of it, are outlined in Chapter Ten.

Crime Does Not Pay

Cliché number three.

Crime is a multi-billion dollar business. It pays significantly in a host of ways. To begin with, the *FBI Uniform Crime Reports* state that nationally, of serious crimes reported, one out of four (24.6 percent) were solved.* Some in prison will admit frankly that they understand the risks of particular forms of crime and accept the exchange of a certain number of years in prison for a standard of living altogether out of reach to them in any form of legitimate employment. If a man's surroundings so limit and confine his horizon of opportunity; if he sees clearly that his racial background, his neighborhood conditions, his limited education all spell permanent poverty and degradation, he will weigh in his mind the price of criminal activity and be tempted to pay it. There is a common saying in prison, "If you can't do the time, don't do the crime." The brute fact is that in comparison to some ways of life, crime *does* pay, and pays well.

Furthermore, crime pays psychologically for those who unconsciously hunger for punishment or structure, as we discussed in the previous section about punishment as a deterrent.

White Collar Crimes

Finally, it is essential to mention that there is a wide area of illegal and highly lucrative criminality that this nation avoids facing directly. The world of fraud, embezzlement, payoffs, and high-level bribery account for unbelievable losses in government, business and industry. Many large firms simply expect and absorb losses from petty cash funds and fraudulent expense accounts. We can never be certain of the amount of theft that remains unreported because a company wishes to avoid bad publicity. The President's Crime Commission reports that in 1965 the major property crimes of

* FBI, *Uniform Crime Reports—1966* (Washington, D.C., United States Government Printing Office, 1967), p. 27. Even more startling is the President's Crime Commission report that estimates between three to ten times more crimes are unreported than those reported. See "The Challenge of Crime on Our Society," pp. 20–21.

robbery, burglary, larceny and auto theft totaled 600 million dollars in economic loss. They estimate the "unreported" commercial theft at 1,400 million dollars—in excess of twice the reported theft.* Embezzlement and fraud (also white collar crimes) total an additional 1,550 million dollars in economic loss. These figures are even more staggering against the background of total crime costs. Our main point is that white collar crime, though highly lucrative, is usually inconspicuous, and rarely investigated or punished by the law. Although the vast majority of the American people are honest, the dishonest citizens who walk in high social and economic circles are not reflected in the prison population to any extent that approaches their number.

We leave the subject of public misunderstanding at this point and take up the topic of law enforcement itself.

Problems With Sentencing

Being a judge is a stupendous responsibility. Few offices demand such intelligence, experience and wisdom. Prison officials see daily the inequality that results from the incredible unevenness in the caliber of judges today. There is a serious crisis in this country's courtrooms.

In recent years, judges (particularly on the Federal level) have been gathered together for "Sentencing Institutes" to study the business of fixing sentences. At one such instituted meeting in Illinois, 54 Federal judges were given a kit containing background data on five convicted offenders: an income tax violator, a youthful offender, a bank robber, a forger, and an embezzler. With identical information before them, the judges were asked to vote on the sentences to be imposed. In the case of the bank robber, the judges voted as follows:

1 for civil commitment to a mental hospital.
1 for commitment to determine competency.
3 for probation with psychiatric care.
28 for diagnostic commitment, for some imprisonment.
14 for prison sentences ranging to 20 years.

* See *op. cit.*, pp. 47–48, for further information on white collar crime.

6 for indeterminate sentences, from five to 20 years.

1 for a 10-year sentence, with a one-year minimum to be served.*

Except for the youthful offender, all the sample situations drew as wide a variety of sentences as did the bank robber.

The problem is all too familiar to those in prison. Judges determine peoples' fates without adequate background information, uniform criteria, and awareness of their own personal biases. Society cannot realistically expect uniform sentences all across the courts of the land. But we do have a right to expect (indeed to demand) a uniform philosophy and procedure for sentencing. Judges have too much power and too little information about those over whom they exercise judgment. Judges receive virtually no formal training or education for their office. In the higher courts their knowledge of the law stems from successful apprenticeship as attorneys. Among the basic tools needed are:

1. Pre-sentence investigation reports.
2. Diagnostic centers, where observation and professional evaluation can offer a much deeper picture of the offender's problems.
3. Consultations with other judges on special situations.
4. Regular in-service training on standards and criteria for imposing sentences.

In the higher courts the above suggestions are vastly complicated by a further problem: lack of time because of overcrowded court dockets.

The issue is typified by the following article in *Time*, June 24, 1966:

An End to Copping Out

The pitch usually goes like this: "The district attorney has you dead to rights. But if you plead guilty to a lesser charge and save the state the time and expense of a trial, I will let you off with a light sentence." The offer comes from a judge. The second party to the bargain is a nervous defendant accused of a crime, almost certain to be convicted, and tempted to "cop a plea." The practice is one of long standing. And it has advantages for the public as well as the accused: it clears crowded dockets and sometimes extracts information about other crimes and other criminals as part of the bargain. But is it proper?

Last week Federal Judge Edward Weinfeld of New York's Southern

* The full report on "Judges Go to School" is found in the magazine section of *New York Times*, November 1966, p. 36.

District answered firmly that judges have no business getting mixed up in such deals. A 65-year-old jurist with a reputation for working long hours and never ducking the tough cases, Weinfeld insisted that the bargain deprives a defendant of his rights without due process, impairs a judge's objectivity, makes a sham of the guilty plea and "has no place in a system of justice."

Such bargains, said Weinfeld, *are inherently wrong* because of "the unequal positions of the judge and the accused, one with the power to commit to prison and the other deeply concerned to avoid prison." *A guilty plea "predicated upon a judge's promise of a definite sentence,"* he added, "by its very nature does not qualify as a free and voluntary act."*

Minor Court Justice

There are 15,000 minor courts in the United States, and about two-thirds of the judges who preside over them are not lawyers. These courts handle traffic offenders, and misdemeanors charges. The pay is usually low, and many of the magistrates work only part time as judges. Their work is unsupervised; their training is minimal. In 32 states justices and judges earn all or part of their money by collecting fees in criminal cases. Such a situation cannot help but encourage the magistrate to find people guilty and heap on costs to make a profit. The magistrate's cut is normally geared to the size of the fine.

We call this to the pastor's attention because progressive legislators are working toward reordering a judge's authority in sentencing. The issues are complex. But the needs are clear. Judges need more tools to carry the weighty responsibility of meting out the form and degree of penalty for criminal activity.

What Can a Minister Do?

Three very specific things:

1. In individual cases, be sure your people have a good lawyer. And make certain the judge sees your interest in the case. Wear your

* There are impressive arguments in favor of this common practice of "negotiated plea." But even the President's Crime Commission report, which supports the practice, agrees that better controls need to be added because of its abuse. See pp. 134–136.

clerics to court. Sit up front. Your very presence in the courtroom will help insure things are done "decently and in order."

2. Know the lawyers of your community—their reputation, their ethics, their clientele. Lend you own weight for the best and honest among them to get into the positions of authority (city council, judge, elected office). Law courts are rough and competetive places. Ambition can be ruthless, and innocent people get caught because they are without money and without an interested advocate.

3. Ninety percent of arrests never go to trial. This means that most decisions are worked out between the suspect, lawyers and judge. Work for the institution of a Legal Aid Society in your neighborhood so that men and their families can get legal advice in time of crisis. Some inner-city churches even establish a legal aid clinic as part of their church programs. The poor can come there for legal advice—free and apart from the pressure of courtroom expediencies.

4. In states where magistrates have no legal training and areas where the judges receive a portion of the court fines, corruption and injustices are almost guaranteed. Find out what is going on.

Trial by Jury

One of the often-questioned elements of our judicial procedure is the jury system. A recent study* offers a number of reassuring indications with regard to the jury system. A thorough ten-year research project reports that in 72 percent of all criminal trials, the judges agree fully with the jury. In only 9 percent does the judge criticize the jury for an improper verdict. This remarkable correlation between the opinion of a professional and a group of laymen is one of many points that testify that the jury system is a reliable and responsible method of deciding innocence and guilt.

Parole Boards

When the parole board comes to the prison, there is an air of tension and anticipation. A parole board has a crucial job. It decides if a prisoner in the midst of serving a required percentage of his

* Harry Kalven, Jr. and Hans Zusel, *The American Jury* (New York: Little, Brown and Company, 1967).

sentence is or is not ready to return to society. A man serving a sentence is obliged by law to complete a certain mandatory percentage of that sentence (usually 2/3 of the minimum sentence). After that period expires, he is "eligible to meet the parole board." At the point where they judge he is at a peak of "readiness," they release him to serve the rest of his sentence "on parole," that is, under legal supervision.

Parole boards grow out of a belief that the prison experience should prepare a man for citizenship some time before the full extent of his sentence is served. The chance for parole seeks to motivate a prisoner to prove himself in prison.

It is important to note that a parole board is society's vehicle for "forgiveness." A man is found guilty and sentenced to imprisonment —let us say for five to fifteen years. After he has completed 2/3 of his minimum sentence (in this case, 3 years and 4 months) he is "eligible" to see the parole board. They then decide on the basis of his previous record, his prison record, and a parole evaluation, if the man "deserves" release. If they decide he does, the man completes the rest of his sentence in society under supervision of a parole officer. He has thus been convicted and punished. But if his punishment proves "rehabilitative," his imprisonment becomes a form of "repentance" that justifies the "forgiveness" of conditional freedom. If he misuses the trust, that is, if he violates his parole, he is returned to the prison to complete his full sentence. Thus, the "forgiveness" is revoked and the full measure of penalty required.

The church, at some level of strength (such as the national and state Councils of Churches), ought to get involved in efforts to make certain that parole boards:

1. Have members who are experienced and qualified.
2. Have a range of membership that includes not only those acquainted with the law, but those conversant in the medical, social and moral disciplines.
3. Have criteria which are predictable and open to review.*

The plain fact is that parole boards, like many appointed offices,

* However the problem of any "review" of a parole board decision is difficult because of the chance of political influence in parole judgments. It is doubtful that individual decisions could be reviewed; but it is the standards and policies for decision-making that need clarification.

often become positions for patronizing and fulfilling political obligations. It is not commonly known that new governors or United States presidents mean new parole boards. The practice of appointing parole commissioners rather than electing them is probably the best approach, but the church can and should insist on standards that will insure that human forgiveness is lodged in the hands of concerned, competent persons. Surely that institution that is centered on the wonderful news of God's love for mankind has a right to know concretely how and who is meting forgiveness for those who have offended society.

Capital Punishment

Nearly all pastors have struggled with the issue of whether or not society is morally justified in executing criminals. Those whose motto is "an eye for an eye and a tooth for a tooth" find no difficulty in justifying "a life for a life."

Of the 50 states, 41 retain capital punishment in some form. The arguments in favor of execution usually boil down to two:

1. Some crimes are irrevocable and their perpetrators cannot be forgiven or restored to freedom. They demand forfeiture of life.
2. Criminals are deterred partly by fear, and capital punishment has the forceful effect of reducing violence in criminal acts.

Some persons say capital punishment can be supported by biblical quotation and has defenders among clergy as well as lawmakers. Supporters of capital punishment point out that it is more humane than the slow disintegration of life imprisonment.

Careful research studies challenge both the chief arguments in its favor. With respect to its deterrent value the President's Crime Commission reports the following:

The most complete study on the subject, based on a comparison of homicide rates in capital and non-capital jurisdictions, concluded that there is no discernible correlation between the availability of the death penalty and the homicide rate. (p. 143)

The study also revealed that the death penalty had no discernible effect on the safety of policemen or prison guards.

In addition studies indicate clearly that the death sentence is imposed disproportionately on the Negro, the poor, and members of unpopular groups. There is little question that money, influence, and background make a critical difference in who is executed and who is not.

Capital punishment is expensive. The courts are fallible and have erred. The death penalty is not a proven deterrent to criminality. The death penalty has universally fallen on the underprivileged and been avoided by persons of means. Such arguments reveal the injustices in administering the ultimate penalty by human courts. But beyond the limitations of the law is a more searching moral issue: does a just society have the right to permanently restrict the life of a member who grievously offends it? Without equivocating, our answer is both "Yes" and "No." Yes, it does, but not by execution. "Yes," because there are persons so dangerous to others and themselves that it is immoral to free them and jeopardize others. Their life must be restricted permanently. "No," because restriction by execution makes the decision too soon. It is clear that some who have committed murder (or treason or kidnapping) do, while in prison, undergo such observable change that their freedom would harm no one. If they were executed, their redemption (or "recovery" or "maturity" or "reform"—depending on one's frame of reference) is preempted and precluded. Morally, the issue is, "Can human beings arrest a person and judge his life to be irredeemable because of the viciousness of his crime?" One belief that runs throughout this book is that little advance will occur in reducing crime until we affirm that the just and humane approach will concentrate on the person in prison *more* than the act which brought him there.

Many will say this is sentimental, soft and unrealistic. They will say, "killers must be killed," ignoring the possibility of an occasional mistaken execution, and ignoring the proven inequalities in applying this straightforward conviction. They will say the law must be feared and obeyed and nothing short of the full penalty can do justice to some crimes. They know the mind of God so clearly, that they can act in His stead, being positive they can judge certain actions as inexcusable and unforgivable. We cannot find any mandate in the teachings of Christ for human kind to discern who will never change, who acts in ways that prove beyond any doubt that he is beyond redemption.

We feel the church has many important legislative battles to fight in besides the matter of capital punishment. The basic battle should not be to abolish capital punishment. The real struggle is with the hearts of men—that still insist on dividing the world and people unequivocably into good and evil, just and unjust.

Summary and Conclusion

Social issues are increasingly laid at the door of the church and the pastor with the urgent demand, "Do something." It is extremely difficult to judge what can be done and what should be done. Pastors know that they inherit a mantle of tradition that is both priestly and prophetic. Most of this volume is directed to guiding the priestly work of those who seek to bind up the brokenhearted, the poor and the imprisoned.

Yet, we have prophetic tasks also—and they are herculean. The grim failure in prison rehabilitation demands explanation. Whoever looks for causes is led into a labyrinth of difficult issues involving not only the prison, but courts, lawyers, judges, legislators and ultimately, society itself.

This is a chapter of judgment and criticism. No pastor can comprehend the problem of prisons and prisoners without some awareness of the massive task it is to effect "liberty and justice for all." We are convinced that the problems suggested in this chapter cannot be faced by pastors as individuals. These are tasks for the church as an organization, and for pastors as ministerial associations. We offer this picture of current and recurrent conflicts in the legal world for two reasons:

1. to acquaint pastors with some of the failures and fallacies that embitter all who are caught by the law, and drive them into further alienation from society and its laws;

2. to offer a *checklist* for any ministerial association or denomination who wishes to inquire into and make evaluation of the caliber of its community's judicial and penal program.

CHAPTER TEN

The HARD ROAD To FREEDOM

Each year over 100,000 adults and 27,000 youths make a precarious move from state and Federal correctional institutions to the "free world." It is a quiet, almost unnoticed transition—except for the turmoil raging inside the released prisoner.

We know the terrific problems that plagued World War II soldiers returning to civilian life. Shell shock, insomnia, neurotic fears and marital strain greeted a host of veterans adjusting to their discharge. Similarly, after surgery, there is a critical period known as postoperative recovery. The patient often has to regain weight, recondition muscles, take rest periods, and perhaps endure some depression. When a man leaves prison there is a period just as critical and precarious as returning from war or recovery. *It takes at least one year for a person who has been locked up to adjust to freedom and responsibility.* Those who serve lengthy sentences—8, 10, 15 years—require longer.

In this chapter, we will use the term "releasee" to refer to the ex-prisoner in the process of adjusting to civilian life. The releasee faces a frightening transition. In prison he was part of his own subculture—alienated from those in authority and separated from those at home. The prison world is now behind; the outside appears strange and hostile. The releasee is caught between two worlds, no longer a part of one, and subtly out of place in the other. To make the adjustment he needs support and acceptance.

The releasee faces the world with a suit of clothes, a $20 bill (the amount varies) and a bus or train ticket home. Whether he enters "the street" on parole or having finished his sentence, his release spells the start of a new kind of trial. Everyone—his family, friends, employer, the police, and most of all, the man himself—apprehensively wonders if he can "make it."

The answer to this question depends fundamentally on what is inside the man. But it also depends on what is outside him. The released prisoner cannot succeed without help.

The Parole Board

Since two out of three releasees are on parole, it is profitable to consider the questions a parole board asks as it evaluates a prisoner's readiness for release.

Basically, the parole board evaluates a man in three areas: (1) his record prior to arrest, (2) his performance in the prison, (3) his resources and capacity to adjust if released.

They must look at a man from within and from without. In the former category, they examine the extent and seriousness of the prisoner's problems before his arrest. Here, the chief source book is the file of records that have been accumulated. Then they must evaluate his progress while confined—his adjustment, attitude, work record, and level of maturity—based on the reports of the prison staff. Finally, they must study the atmosphere which awaits him and his ability to adjust to the waiting world. This is the point where a pastor and church comes in. Consider the questions a parole board asks itself in terms of a prisoner's community resources:

1. Will he go home to a family? What kind of family is it? A wife and children? Parents? An aunt and uncle? No one?
2. Does he have any savings?
3. What kind of job will he have? His old job? A new job? What is he trained to do?
4. Where will he live when he gets out? What kind of neighborhood and environment?
5. Does he have any friends? What kind of people are they? How well has he kept in touch with those on the outside? Is anyone sponsoring or taking special interest in the prisoner?

These questions point to the areas where pastors and churches can offer guidance and direction of great value.

Finding Jobs

When a man leaves prison, he needs a job. If he has been confined for long, he may have savings from the prison amounting to one or two hundred dollars. Such capital will not last long. Authorities usually require an inmate to have an approved job before he is released. That is not easy. Sometimes men in prison will write 200 to 300 job applications begging for employment. Often it is an exercise in futility. But all avenues are not blocked. Frequently state employment agencies are a great help in locating employment.

A man in prison needs an "advocate," someone who will make personal contact with an employer to obtain him a job. Most often, this is done by a man's relatives. Frequently, men have no close relatives or they are so separated from them, they can not get help from home. Securing him a job is one tangible way in which churchmen can help a released prisoner.

Finding Residence

A married man will return to his family if his home has remained intact. An earlier chapter explored the church's role with families, step by step. But suppose (it often happens) a man's wife leaves him? Or suppose the prisoner is unmarried? Then where does he go to live? Most men simply find a room—enduring emptiness and loneliness with nowhere to turn.

Halfway houses.   One alternative to living alone is the "halfway house" A plan begun in the 1950s, the halfway house is a staffed residence where men newly released from prison live under guidance. It takes into account the host of obstacles of prisoners when released: their fear of society; their isolation; their need for support in the gradual adjustment to normal responsibilities; and their need for a welcome place to call "home." The halfway house concept underscores the fact that freedom is frightening, and must be shouldered in regulated doses.

It offers a bridge between the institutional life of total dependency and the severe demands of independent responsibility. A man works in the community but lives in the house with other releasees who are at different stages in the same process of adjustment. He uses his free time as he wishes but group meetings offer him the chance to talk out fears and frustrations that daily accompany him.

Several groups and agencies run halfway houses. Most of them are in large cities. Federally-operated halfway houses are called "Pre-Release Guidance Centers." Currently, they are concentrating on youthful offenders (under age 27). An early and notably successful church-run halfway house is St. Leonard's House in Chicago, begun in 1954. It is an agency of the Episcopal Diocese of Chicago.

Ministers should know about and support the halfway house movement. At the time of this writing, halfway houses can be found in only five of the fifty states. Some churches, particularly in the cities, may have the resources for starting a halfway house. Inner-city churches not equipped to operate one themselves can offer to help— with money, space and volunteers—a secular halfway house.* And the pastor who wants to help a single prisoner (particularly a young offender) find a place to live should check on the possibility of a halfway house. A good one offers much more than a place to sleep. It offers counseling, job placement, social life and a community for those facing common obstacles.

The Parishioner and the Parolee

Another movement, still in embryonic stages, is the use of concerned church laymen who become acquainted with men in prison and continue the relationship after the inmate is released.

As we noted earlier, men released on parole serve the remainder of their sentence under supervision of a parole officer. In Massachusetts, an imaginative prison chaplain has inspired church members to work in conjunction with him and parole officers. Most parole officers carry very heavy caseloads. Their relationship with the releasee is strained because the parole officer has the power to "violate" (that is, recommend the court return a man to prison for infractions in the terms of his parole**). However, a mature layman, given training and consultation, can augment the role of a parole officer.

The program is known as the Protestant Fellowship. Twice weekly, "outmates," visitors representing fifty various churches, meet in small discussion groups with inmates at the state prison. Relation-

* It may be of interest to know the Federal Government, through the poverty program, will award money to agencies, including churches, that have approved staff and program for a halfway house.
** For instance, an ex-prisoner violates parole if he leaves the area, changes jobs, or moves his residence without permission. He violates parole if he has contact with anyone with an arrest record, or bothers a wife from whom he is separated.

ships are established inside and may continue after the inmate is released. On the outside, regional meetings are held for fellowship and discussion of personal problems. Ex-inmates and outmates meet together with churches to share their experiences in the Protestant Fellowship. When a friendship develops between an outmate and an ex-inmate, it is supervised by the chaplain and the man's parole officer.

Programs such as the Protestant Fellowship require exceptional cooperation between a department of correction, the chaplain, the department of parole and the local churches. Training, supervision and controls are essential to its success. In the chaplain's brochure of instructions to outmates is the following clear statement:

Because of security requirements inside the institution and parole restrictions outside, outmates carry on relationships within specified limits and in constant communication with Chaplain Dutton, who is responsible for actions of outmates, both in the institution and in their relationships with parolees.*

What Pastors Can Do

As a pastor or layman works with the released inmate, we would repeat one important thought. The first year out of prison is the most crucial period. This is the time of fears, failures, desperation and disappointment that lead back to prison. It was Joe's first day out of prison and he headed for home filled with joy. He discovered his wife living with another man. He beat up the man, went out and got drunk. The next morning, he failed to report to his parole officer, was found drunk in an alley and returned to prison for violation of parole. He was fortunate not to face new charges for assault.

"Freedom," observes Eric Fromm, "can be terrifying if it is not accompanied by assured confidence and clarity of destination." We cannot overemphasize the fragile, precarious extent of the early period of a releasee's freedom. When the gate swings open, the releasee confronts countless decisions which he has not made for some time—what he will eat, when he will retire, how to handle his money and his sexual drives.

* For further information on "The Protestant Fellowship," contact Chaplain Robert L. Dutton, Box 43, Norfolk, Massachusetts 02056.

Many former prisoners simply cannot cope with too much freedom and too little structure. What might a pastor do to assist the releasee during these difficult days?

—Meet him at the prison or the train or bus depot on release. You take the first step toward him in the outside world. Invite him to take the next toward you.

—Make specific appointments for him to come to your office: to talk, to drain tension, to discuss problems, to acknowledge fears, and to regard the church as a "place" of refuge and concern. Suggest four or five meetings the first two weeks. Then meet weekly for a while.

—Talk with him honestly and openly about ways he can restrain and contain his fears and impulses.

—Discuss participation in groups with him. He needs groups; he needs obligations; he needs help getting back into social settings and recovering his poise. Alcoholics often find in Alcoholics Anonymous a genuine lifeline back to respectability. In fact, A.A. people will meet any alcoholic inmate at the gate and take him to his first meeting. Yokefellows is another excellent group offering support and acceptance.

—Ask for some help from him. Offer him the chance to *give* to you or the Church. He might paint a classroom, fold worship bulletins weekly, or serve on a committee.

His letters from prison may tell you eloquently how he longs to have a new chance to make things right, to take care of his family, to start a new life. Yet, all that is neurotic in him will entice him to invent some way to ruin his lovely dreams and hopes. Do not be timid about building some fences (such as weekend commitments) around him as he comes out. One side of him may chafe and resist because he has come to hate fences. Another side of him will be silently thankful because a fence does not just hold things in; it also holds things together.

What Is Ahead in Correction Work?

A great deal. There are signs of creative ferment among legislators and penologists. In 1965 President Johnson established a Crime Study Commission that has produced the most carefully detailed study of crime ever undertaken in America. The recommendations of the President's Crime Commission confirms the worth of several embryonic programs and helps us predict the direction penology is taking.

Some State legislatures have authorized significant revisions of their penal code. Some jail territories have developed work-release programs that require short-term offenders (misdemeanor charges) to hold down their normal jobs during the day and "check into" jail at night for the prescribed sentence. Judges, acknowledging the complexities of sentencing, have begun to develop "sentencing school workshops" to improve their judgment in imposing sentences.

Diversification of institutions has begun to separate first offenders from hardened repeaters; remove mental defectives from normal prison population; and confine those with physical handicaps—tuberculosis, epilepsy, etc.—to institutions with better medical facilities. Youth camps and vocational training centers are offering significant efforts to work with youthful offenders in an atmosphere of less restraint and greater responsibility.

Amidst the ferment of American penology today several programs are representative of the effort to restrain prisoners yet ameliorate the abnormal atmosphere which so stifles motivation for change. We will discuss two such efforts—the "work release" and the "home furlough" program. Such programs represent a movement to strengthen a prisoner's work habits and family ties while he serves his sentence.

Work-Release Programs

The Prisoner Rehabilitation Act, passed last fall, is the most significant legislative reform in modern American penology. Hundreds of prisoners already are working in daytime jobs as they finish their sentences at night. They are learning job skills that will bring dignity to themselves and support to their families.—President Johnson (March 9, 1966)

In Chapter Four, we described the grinding, dehumanizing process of institutionalization. Its great danger is that a man loses self-respect and with it his incentive to improve. A few prisons and jails have begun releasing prisoners to work in nearby communities and return to the prison after work. The following letter from an employer helps explain why work release programs are valuable:

I won't hire ex-convicts. I don't care if a convict has paid his debt to society. I don't care if he ever owed a debt to society. He has spent a number of years in the packed, unhealthy, plotting atmosphere of the penitentiary. I owe too much to the men I already have in my plant. This man won't do for my plant. He has had the initiative ground out of him. He has lost the sense of pride in productive work. His mind is teeming with ideas that he may not have accepted fully, but he cannot purge these from his brain because he was forced to live upon them for lack of other nourishment. He has been trained to intrigue and to conspire for even the simplest things that other men take for granted—tobacco, reading matter, a few extra minutes of conversation. These arguments pile up indefinitely—a solid array of facts. I address my challenge not to the prisoners, but to the nation. Keep your convicts or make citizens out of them. No man should serve a sentence and then step out into the world. There should be a period of preparation. If society's debt must be paid to the hilt, then add some time for real rehabilitation.*

Pastors can help immeasurably by interpreting to their congregations the rationale of the "work-release" program. Work-release programs represent an effort to test out realistically a prisoner's readiness to return to responsible citizenship. The real working world simply cannot be simulated within the institutional world. A community takes a giant step in aiding the rehabilitation of a prisoner when it accepts the release work program for men from nearby prisons. Here are a few of the psychological gains of a prisoner released daily to work in the community:

1. He is trusted. He must work without any guards watching his his actions and checking his self-control.
2. He can support his own family, instead of having them live on welfare.
3. He must compete on the open market, giving a day's work for a day's wage. Discipline, reliability and performance are essential traits in each job, and challenge some men that have never before had such incentive to prove themselves.

Trust, dignity, responsibility and tested performance are com-

* From *The Harbinger*, Kansas State Industrial Reformatory, October 1962.

modities a penal institution simply cannot realistically offer within its walls. And these are precisely the stuff rehabilitation is made of. Some prisoners will fail the test. They will abuse the trust and bring criticism to the system. But their failures will be detected quicker and earlier than parole supervision can do, and each failure will give tangible evidence of a man unprepared for parole.

Of the hundreds of prisons in the United States, only a handful have developed a work-release program. The first obstacle is prison officials themselves, who view their obligation to confine men as so fundamental that they will not risk criticism or jeopardize security to pursue such an effort. One cannot blame them as long as a naive public demands a man "pay the full penalty" and screams at the possibility of dangerous criminals on the loose. Such fears are simply unfounded because over 127,000 "dangerous criminals" are released each year, and in fact two thirds of those who are under the care of the correctional department are outside the walls (that is, on parole) rather than inside. The second obstacle lies in community education, because certainly shops and factories will not be persuaded to employ men serving a prison sentence unless they understand the excellent safeguards built into such programs. Nationwide programs to "hire the handicapped" have demonstrated that physically handicapped workers have exceptional incentive to do good work. Few men who enter a community for nine hours each day and then return to a prison cell for the next fifteen are going to jeopardize the chance to face a parole board and hear the words, "You did well for 9 hours a day. We think you are ready to try for 24."

Perhaps even more controversial than work-release programs is the practice of giving prisoners furloughs. The obvious purpose in allowing prisoners home furloughs is to strengthen ties with a family. One form of this program is allowing selected prisoners a weekend furlough to be home with their family. An alternative approach is that some prisons arrange rooms within the institution in which couples can be alone. Both approaches present administrative problems and require additional forms of screening and supervising. The goal, however, is sound. To make genuine progress in the complicated work of helping people change, there must be positive sources of motivation. The traditional warning of "keep your nose clean and you'll get out" simply does not accomplish the higher goal of seeing to it that the prisoner who is released has found greater resources to cope with life once he does get out.

These, then, are a few of the major movements in penology. Research into antisocial behavior is only in embryonic stages. Certain crimes—notably sex offenses and murder—have undergone considerable study. But the vast majority of men who go to prison are neither understood nor significantly helped. The road ahead for both prisons and prisoners is better marked and encouraging; but it is still long and arduous.

CHAPTER ELEVEN

COUNSELING PRINCIPLES

Good counseling is an art, but the underlying skills are developed with properly-supervised experience. Three principles, which apply in all counseling, take on added importance in work with inmates.

The Infinite Value of Careful, Attentive Listening

The life of a prisoner is utterly jammed with others telling him what he should do, what he should want, should plan for, and should be. Listening attentively to the man in prison is urgent because his world is replete with people telling him what is best for him and what to do.

Junior, who is 22, was stealing cars in the city. He went to prison and served 18 months. His mother begged him to come back and live at home. His parole officer urged him to get out of the city and away from home. Nobody really knew what Junior wanted. Neither did Junior. Nobody listened long enough or probed deeply enough to help him find out.

In no setting more than a prison is a man's life so completely under the domination of authorities. All too often the decisions about a prisoner's future are arbitrary, hasty, repressive and unrealistic. A man spends five years in prison for a sexual offense. He goes before the parole board and hears, "We see you are a dance instructor. Mixing with the entertainment crowd is bad for you. No more dancing for the next five years while you are on parole." "But dancing is my vocation, it's my life." "You should have thought about that before. . . ."

Such decisions often represent puritanical, unrealistic nonsense. If the man has sexual problems, restricting him from the entertainment field will do nothing to help resolve them. Instead, such continued, subtle forms of punishment will merely enlarge his frustration and sharpen his hostility to a world that will not accept him.

But the main point is that to a man who is *told* what is best for him from the length of his prison sentence to the conditions of his parole, a pastor who will help him discern what he truly wants for himself represents a rare figure.

Keep Initiative with the Man

One of the worst problems of confinement to an institution is that a man becomes dependent on it. The danger of an existence in which every moment is planned and regimented is that one soon forgets how to make decisions for oneself. In such situations, the prisoner tends to feel helpless and conveys his helplessness in ways that tempt the pastor to take care of him. A vital principle in all counseling is to help the man take responsibility for his own actions, his own decisions and his own life. Two short vignettes illustrate this point:

BILL: "Pastor, I see the parole board in two months. Can you find me a job so I'll be ready if they let me go?"

PASTOR: "Sure, I'll be glad to help. Will you write up a summary for me of your interests and experience. Mention places where you have worked before. Then I will have something to work with–OK?"

BILL: "Aw, just anything you come up with will suit me fine, Reverend. I'm not fussy."

It is tough for a prisoner to obtain a job simply by correspondence. So he is justified in asking the pastor for help. But there should be built into the pastor's reply, the opportunity for the man to make a contribution and feel in some way he is representing himself. Don't do things for a man he can do for himself. If he knows how to write, give him the chance to formulate a good introductory letter and a detailed employment summary.

BILL: "Chaplain, will you write my wife for me? Tell her I am sorry the parole board turned me down this year. I can't face her myself."

CHAPLAIN: "Bill, it's rough to break bad news, isn't it? Kind of like failing again. How do you think she will take it?"

At the start, the chaplain must recognize this man's call for help in dealing with a wife who anxiously awaits word that he will soon be home. And that is the counseling focus. But the letter should come from the man. It is his wife; it is their mutual disappointment, and he needs to face it. The constant temptation to the pastor is to do things for people that unwittingly deny them the chance to learn how to do things for themselves.

Be Careful Not to Over-Identify with the Prisoner

In the field of counseling, a faculty that truly separates the professional from the novice is the capacity to remain objective—to keep perspective. Great concern for a person so easily generates the need to protect him and please him. The prisoner is often deeply entrenched in the belief that all people are phony and nobody cares. In fact, that is the pervasive atmosphere in prisons. A result is the powerful drive to test people: "How far will he go for me?" "How much will he believe me?" "How much can I get from him before he will give up on me?"

A certain amount of testing is expected in all counseling relationships—"Will the pastor spend more than an hour with me?" "Is the pastor going to reject me if I tell him how I really feel?" And unconsciously, "What will it take by way of demands for me to prove to myself I'm really too bad for anyone to love?" In counseling with prisoners, the testing is usually quite pronounced.

BILL: "It was great of you to come. You're the only visitor I've had for three months. Would you come every week?"

PASTOR: "I enjoyed the talk too, Bill, but my schedule is just too crowded to get up here that often. We can get a lot of talking done through the mail and I'll let you know when I can come back again."

The inmate may be quite right that no one does visit him. And hearing this call for attention, the pastor can take a clue to see what is the barrier between him and his wife, or other relatives who are not visiting. Or he may talk with a man in the church who could arrange to visit regularly. But unless he is a most unusual pastor, it is unlikely he could keep a commitment of weekly visits for one, two, five or ten years. Hence, to make an unrealistic promise is to insure failure later on and reinforce the inmate's worst fear—that nobody can be trusted for very long.

The pastor's tools must always be adapted to the age and setting in which he ministers to people. But his unchanging role is to present the law of God through his own uniquely human personality. Wherever the pastor enters the world of crime, courts and criminals he treads strange and difficult ground. If in the midst of five million persons who are arrested every year a pastor can understand and reach out to one such man it will be a gift of grace. We conclude with cautious words because it seems imperative that a pastor realize he cannot work effectively by himself. Many other people are essential to the successful work with those in and out of correctional institutions. Lawyers, churchmen, agencies, chaplains, parole officers, counselors, and many others working together can make the difference in leading a man out of the wilderness of human punishments back to the promise of a new life.

APPENDIX

Crime Capsule*

Almost 3¼ million serious crimes reported during 1966; an 11 percent rise over 1965.

Risk of becoming a victim of serious crime increased 10 percent in 1966, with almost 2 victims per each 100 inhabitants.

Firearms used to commit more than 6,500 murders, and 43,500 aggravated assaults in 1966.

Daytime burglaries of residences rose 140 percent in 1966 over 1960.

Property worth more than $1.2 billion lost as a result of 153,400 robberies, 1,370,000 burglaries, 2,790,000 larcenies, and 557,000 auto thefts. Police recoveries, however, reduced this loss by 55 percent.

Arrest of juveniles for serious crimes increased 54 percent in 1966 over 1960, while number of persons in the young age group, 10–17, increased 19 percent.

Arrests for Narcotic Drug Law violations rose 82 percent, 1960–1966.

Narcotic arrests 1966 over 1965 up 28 percent influenced primarily by marijuana arrests in Western States.

Police solution of serious crimes declined 8 percent in 1966.

Fifty-seven law enforcement officers murdered by felons in 1966. Firearms used as murder weapons in 96 percent of police killings since 1960.

* FBI, *Uniform Crime Reports—1966* (Washington, D.C.: Government Printing Office, 1967). p. 1. If you wish assistance in the interpretation of any information in this publication, you may communicate with the Director, Federal Bureau of Investigation, United States Department of Justice, Washington, D.C. 20535.

Careers in Crime: Study disclosed 55 percent of offenders released to the streets in 1963 rearrested within two and one-half years.

Fifty-seven percent of the offenders released on parole were rearrested within 2½ years.

Sixty-seven percent of prisoners released early in 1963 after earning "good time" were rearrested.

Eighty-three percent of those persons acquitted or dismissed in 1963 were rearrested within 30 months.

Seventy-two percent of persons granted probation in 1963 for auto theft repeated in a new crime.

Of the young offenders under 20 released in 1963, 65 percent repeated.

Mobility study reveals over 60 percent of the repeaters charged with robbery, burglary, auto theft, sex offenses and forgery were rearrested in two or more states during their criminal careers.

1966 police employee rate of 2 police employees per 1,000 population was first change since 1960.

BIBLIOGRAPHY

Amos, Ed. D., William E., Raymond L. Manella and Marilyn A. Southwell. *Action Programs for Delinquency Prevention.* Springfield, Illinois: Charles C Thomas, 1965.

Amos, William E. and Raymond L. Manella. *Delinquent Children in Juvenile Correctional Institutions.* Springfield, Illinois: Charles C Thomas, 1966.

Amos, William E. and Charles F. Wellford. *Delinquency Prevention: Theory and Practice.* Englewood Cliffs, New Jersey: Prentice-Hall, Inc., 1967.

Brennan, James J. and Donald W. Olmstead. *Police Work with Delinquents: Analysis of a Training Program.* East Lansing: Social Science Research Bureau, Michigan State University, 1965.

Bromberg, M.D., Walter. *Crime and the Mind.* New York: The Macmillan Company, 1965.

Capote, Truman. *In Cold Blood.* New York: Random House, 1966.

Cavan, Ruth Shonle. *Readings in Juvenile Delinquency.* Philadelphia: J. B. Lippincott Co., 1964.

Cohen, Albert K. *Deviance and Control.* Englewood Cliffs, New Jersey: Prentice-Hall, Inc., 1966.

Conrad, John. *Crime and Its Correction.* Berkeley: University of California Press, 1965.

Craft, Michael. *Psychopathic Disorders.* Long Island City: Pegamon Press, 1966.

DiSalle, Michael V. *The Power of Life or Death.* New York: Random House, 1965.

Dressler, David. *Readings in Criminology and Penology.* New York: Columbia University Press, 1964.

Eldefonso, Edward. *Law Enforcement and the Youthful Offender: Juvenile Procedures.* New York: John Wiley & Sons, Inc., 1967.

Feldman, Frances Lomas and Frances H. Scherz. *Family Social Welfare: Helping Troubled Families.* New York: Atherton Press, 1967.

133

FENTON, NORMAN, ERNEST G. REIMER, and HARRY A. WILMER. *The Correctional Community: An Introduction and Guide*. Berkeley: University of California Press, 1967.

FRIEDLAND, MARTIN L. *Detention Before Trial: A Study of Criminal Cases Tried in the Toronto Magistrates' Courts*. Toronto: University of Toronto Press, 1965.

GIALLOMBARDO, ROSE. *Juvenile Delinquency: A Book of Readings*. New York: John Wiley & Sons, Inc., 1966.

GOLD, HARRY and FRANK R. SCARPITTI. *Combatting Social Problems: Techniques of Intervention*. New York: Holt, Rinehart, and Winston, 1967.

GWYN, ALLEN H. *Work, Earn and Save: Observations on Crime and Correction*. Institute for Civic Education, Extension Division, University of North Carolina, Chapel Hill, 1963.

HESS, ALBERT G. *The Young Adult Offender*. New York: United Nations, 1965.

JEFFERY, C. R. *Criminal Responsibility and Mental Disease*. Springfield Illinois: Charles C Thomas, Publisher, 1967.

JONES, HOWARD. *Crime in a Changing Society*. Baltimore: Penguin Books, 1965.

KEISER, R. *Hustler: Henry Williamson. The Autobiography of a Thief*. New York: Doubleday & Company, Inc., 1965.

KNOPKA, GISELA. *The Adolescent Girl in Conflict*. Englewood Cliffs, N.J.: Prentice-Hall, Inc., 1966.

KRASNER, LEONARD and LEONARD P. ULLMANN. *Research in Behavior Modification*. New York: Holt, Rinehart and Winston, Inc., 1966.

KVARACEUS, WILLIAM C. *Anxious Youth: Dynamics of Delinquency*. Columbus: Charles E. Merrill Books, Inc., 1966.

LEWIS, PH.D., ORLANDO F. *The Development of American Prisons and Prison Customs, 1776–1845*. Montclair, N.J.: Patterson Smith, 1967.

LUNDEN, WALTER A. *The Prison Warden and the Custodial Staff*. Springfield, Illinois: Charles C Thomas, 1965.

MacDOUGALL, CURTIS D. *The Press and Its Problems*. Dubuque: William C. Brown Company, 1965.

MacIVER, ROBERT M. *The Prevention and Control of Delinquency*. New York: Atherton Press, 1966.

MacLEOD, ALASTAIR W. *Recidivism: A Deficiency Disease*. Philadelphia: University of Pennsylvania Press, 1965.

MARTIN, JOHN M. and JOSEPH P. FITZPATRICK. *Delinquent Behavior: A Redefinition of the Problem*. New York: Random House, 1965.

MILLER, DEREK. *Growth to Freedom: The Psychosocial Treatment of Delinquent Youth.* Bloomington: Indiana University Press, 1965.

MORRIS, PAULINE. *Prisoners and Their Families.* London: George Allen and Unwin, Ltd., 1965.

PLAYFAIR, GILES and DERRICK SINGTON. *Crime, Punishment and Cure.* London: Secker & Warburg, Ltd., 1965.

POWERS, EDWIN. *Crime and Punishment in Early Massachusetts.* Boston: Beacon Press, 1966.

Proceedings of the Ninety-fifth Annual Congress of Correction of the American Correctional Association, Boston, Mass. Washington, D.C.: American Correctional Association, 1966.

QUAY, HERBERT C. *Juvenile Delinquency: Research and Theory.* New Jersey: D. Van Nostrand Company, Inc., 1965.

QUAY, HERBERT C. *Juvenile Delinquency.* Princeton, N.J.: D. Van Nostrand Company, Inc., 1965.

RADZINOWICZ, LEON. *Ideology and Crime.* New York: Columbia University Press, 1966.

Report of the President's Crime Commission, "The Challenge of Crime in a Free Society," Washington, D.C.: U.S. Government Printing Office, 1967.

RICHMOND, MARK S. *Prison Profiles.* New York: Oceana Publications, Inc., 1965.

ROBINS, LEE N. *Deviant Children Grown Up: A Sociological and Psychiatric Study of Sociopathic Personality.* Baltimore: Williams & Wilkins Co., 1966.

RUBENFELD, SEYMOUR. *Family of Outcasts.* New York: The Free Press, 1965.

SCHAEFER, WALTER V. *The Suspect and Society: Criminal Procedure & Converging Constitutional Doctrines.* Evanston, Illinois: Northwestern University Press, 1967.

SCHOFIELD, MICHAEL. *Sociological Aspects of Homosexuality: A Comparative Study of Three Types of Homosexuals.* Boston: Little, Brown & Company, 1965.

SHERIDAN, WILLIAM H. *Standards for Juvenile and Family Courts.* Washington, D.C.: U.S. Government Printing Office, 1966.

SHOHAM, SHLOMO. *Crime and Social Deviation.* Chicago: Henry Regnery Company, 1966.

SKOLNICK, JEROME H. *Justice without Trial: Law Enforcement in Democratic Society.* New York: John Wiley & Sons, Inc., 1966.

SLAVSON, S. R. *Reclaiming the Delinquent.* New York: The Free Press, 1965.

STERNE, RICHARD S. *Delinquent Conduct and Broken Homes.* New Haven, Conn.: College and University Press Services, Inc., 1964.

STREET, DAVID, ROBERT D. VINTER, and CHARLES PERROW. *Organization for Treatment: A Comparative Study of Institutions for Delinquents.* New York: The Macmillan Company, 1966.

TAFT, DONALD R. and RALPH W. ENGLAND, JR. *Criminology* (4th Edition). New York: The Macmillan Co., 1964.

The Young Adult Offender: A Review of Current Practices and Programmes in Prevention and Treatment. New York: United Nations, 1965.

TOMPKINS, DOROTHY CAMPBELL. *White Collar Crime—A Bibliography.* Berkeley: Institute of Governmental Studies, University of California, 1967.

WARD, DAVID A. and GENE G. KASSEBAUM. *Women's Prison: Sex and Social Structure.* Chicago: Aldine Publishing Company, 1965.

WESTON, PAUL B. and KENNETH M. WELLS. *The Administration of Justice.* Englewood Cliffs, N.J.: Prentice-Hall, Inc., 1967.

WILKENS, LESLIE T. *Social Deviance: Social Policy, Action and Research.* Englewood Cliffs, N.J.: Prentice-Hall, Inc., 1965.

WOLFGANG, MARVIN E. and FRANCO FERRACUTI. *The Subculture of Violence: Towards an Integrated Theory in Criminology.* New York: Barnes & Noble, Inc., 1967.

INDEX